# JESUS IS LORD

JESUS IS LORD

# Jesus Is Lord

## WILFRID TUNINK,
### O.S.B.

1979
Doubleday & Company, Inc.
Garden City, New York

ISBN: 0-385-14793-7
Copyright © 1979 by St. Pius X Abbey, Inc.

LIBRARY OF CONGRESS CATALOG CARD NUMBER 78–19317
ALL RIGHTS RESERVED
PRINTED IN THE UNITED STATES OF AMERICA
FIRST EDITION

# FOREWORD

*Jesus Is Lord* is a unique book, unique in message and unique in genesis. Every search for God is a unique enterprise and every search by God for a beloved servant is a unique journey.

*Jesus Is Lord* is the record of such a double search. In it Father Wilfrid Tunink shares with us the pursuit of his Benedictine vocation "to seek God" and God's pursuit of him, so well expressed by Saint Benedict in his Rule: "What could be sweeter to us than the voice of the Lord inviting us? Behold, in His loving kindness the Lord shows the way of life."

Sacred Scripture is a biography of Jesus. It is, therefore, also a biography of each of His members. Father Wilfrid has found his biography in Sacred Scripture. It is his hope that this discovery will help you find your biography. Salvation history is repeated uniquely in the life of every Christian. The whole of salvation history can be found in the Savior, in all of the saved, and in each of the saved. Read *Jesus Is Lord*, and then find your own biography in God's Word.

I am convinced that this book is destined for a distinct role in the renewal of Christian life. We witness today a growing hunger for intimacy with God through His Word. At the same time that Word is being misinterpreted by a new fundamentalism. This book can help to satisfy the hunger and protect against the deceptions of fundamentalism.

*Jesus Is Lord* came to be in a unique way. It is a community publication of the monastic community of St. Pius X Abbey and its larger community of friends, retreatants, and benefactors.

St. Pius X Abbey was founded to promote especially the renewal of Christian family life. Its founders envisioned this as happening through the spoken word in liturgical prayer, retreat conferences, lectures, and family counseling. But from the beginning it was hoped that the spoken word would be complemented by the written word to be spread through a Family Life Bookstore and the literary efforts of the monks.

*Jesus Is Lord* is one realization of this goal. Through the encouragement and generosity of such friends as Mr. and Mrs. Charles Moll and Mr. and Mrs. Paul Philipp, a staff was formed to prepare this manuscript. The staff consists of Mr. James Richter, design consultant and illustrator; Sister Marie Daugherty, O.P., literary editor; and various members of St. Pius X Abbey, especially Rev. Anselm Ginter, O.S.B., and Brother Dismas Drees, O.S.B., as consultants and critics; and myself as editor-in-chief.

*Maur Burbach, O.S.B.*

# CONTENTS

JESUS IS LORD

# INTRODUCTION

"I will instruct you and teach you the way you should go; I will give you counsel with my eye upon you."[1] I used this verse to decorate the formula of my monastic profession made on September 1, 1941. I recall no special reason why I chose this text from Scripture. I did not then realize how directly and personally the Lord would fulfill the promise of this text in my life. Nor had I any idea of the lengths to which the heavenly Father would go to make me aware of His presence and His love. But this Scripture promise has become my text. It is the word the Lord Jesus has spoken to me, the word He has fulfilled in my regard.

As I look back over my years as a Benedictine monk since that day of my profession, what do I see? There are notable accomplishments, worthwhile achievements. There are times of great peace and joy. But I also see a man filled with turmoil, a man yearning for inner peace and a greater fullness of life. I see a man straining with every fiber of his being to shed the turmoil of

[1] Ps. 31(32):8, the Grail Translation: Joseph Gelineau, *The Psalms: Singing Version* (New York: Paulist Press, Deus Books, 1968). The numbering of the psalms in the Grail Translation follows that of the Vulgate, used also in the Douay Version; in quoting from it, I have also given in parentheses the corresponding psalm numbers used in the Jerusalem Bible and many other versions.

anguish and seeking the freedom of an integrated personality. I see the Lord breaking through and rescuing this man from his straining just when he seemed defeated and crushed by his reactions to the circumstances of life. With that advent of God into his life, his creative energies were awakened. A faith that had almost died began to revive. Another exodus had begun, a very personal one, yet one as real and historical as the first which affected a whole people. The journey has had its mountains and its valleys; it is a journey that will not end with this life. It is a journey which, like that of the Israelites of old, brings me daily into the experience that Jesus is Lord, indeed, *my* Lord. And so I am convinced that it is Jesus who daily says to me, "I will instruct you and teach you the way you should go; I will give you counsel with my eye upon you."

This story brings me no honor or glory, for it tells the love and mercy of Jesus for me. It extols His power and fidelity to His pledged word. It is the story of how He, having chosen me, revealed Himself to me as God-with-me. It shows how I came to know the Father through His gift to Jesus of His own Lordship and through Jesus' gift to me of His Spirit. The story reveals how the Lord God did indeed keep His eye upon me. He came into my life to bring me health of mind and peace of heart. He instructed me in the secrets of His love. He showed me the plan He had for my life. Above all, He let me know Jesus in the gentle power of His Lordship.

By 1965 I had been a monk twenty-four years. Twelve of these were spent at Conception Abbey, where I had received my monastic training. The other twelve I had lived with Conception's daughter house, St. Pius X Monastery in Pevely, Missouri. I was sent there as its second prior in September 1952, a position I resigned on June 1, 1964.

Relief from the responsibilities of being the superior of a young and struggling community brought a temporary sense of freedom and joy. But by November 1965 I found myself the helpless victim of my unconscious energies. I was somewhat prepared for what was happening to me. I had read extensively the works of Carl Jung. I had come to appreciate the role of the unconscious in the maturation process of the human person. I knew that the waves of emotion that flooded me were the released repressions of earlier years. Freed from the need as superior to play any role, I gave these repressions an open, unguarded door; and out they came!

To co-operate with the healing energies of the unconscious surging within, I experimented with the psychological technique of twilight imaging developed by Ira Progoff, Jung's disciple. In this technique one tries to bring the energy of the unconscious under some degree of control and then give it direction. For me this resulted in a very meaningful attempt to integrate the energy of my unconscious into the formation of a richer and stronger personality. Over a period of three years I dreamt regularly. Each dream became a "teaching," through which my unconscious was telling my conscious self what was or would be transpiring. As the Lord used dreams to call and guide people of old, so through these dreams joined with the conscious process of twilight imaging the Lord was instructing me and teaching me the way I should go.

Questions arose: Why was I in this condition? What was the cause of my psychic state? Where did the problems originate? In agony I searched for answers; in pain I had to accept answers. I found them where everyone has to find them—in the unique dynamic of life in my own family. I found them especially in my relationship with my father. I saw clearly that because of his erratic, authoritarian, and explosive character I had never achieved any identification with him. I realized that the only way I overcame fears of my dad was by seeking his approval through hard work and total agreement. Never was I able to express personal views which disagreed with his. A pattern of repression, therefore, was begun. I was irritated and angry at his failure ever to approve my industry. I was frustrated by his outbursts of anger and stubbornness. These feelings were sealed in and were constantly driven deeper into my psyche.

What life at home had become, my pre–Vatican II religious training and my experiences as prior of a small monastic community only confirmed. But this pattern of repression was jolted and shattered rather suddenly when, after my resignation as prior, my unconscious erupted. It was seeking redress for the wrong inflicted upon it. Happily, the technique of repression no longer offered asylum. Other constructive ways of coping with the emotions of the unconscious had to be found. Twilight imaging brought me, initially, into some of these ways.

The healing process thus initiated became a journey for my ego into the regions of the unconscious. This journey often left me helpless. There were moments of panic as I faced powers that seemed satanic. The inner turmoil was reflected in outward behavior. Impulsiveness marked much of my activity. Relationships with confreres were tense and fearful; all humor and gaiety were gone. Often I wrestled with the throes of depression as hostile feelings surged into consciousness and attached themselves to some confrere as a justifying object. I feared authority; but what I feared even more was nonacceptance by those in authority, by confreres, and by people generally. This very fear of rejection drove me to seek acceptance through agreement and co-operation. I suffered deeply through imagination a rejection by my own religious brothers. The pain was so great that I chose the easy way out: withdrawal into sullen aloneness. Added to the painful revelations of the unconscious was the mental and physical exhaustion resulting from many years of overwork. The need to seek approval through hard work still gripped my whole being. It often drove me beyond the point of endurance.

Even in prayer (when one would expect moments of genuine freedom) my attention to the Lord was often swept away by a stream of unconscious thoughts, emotions, and happenings. The struggle was constant and unrelenting, day and night. At times the hostile feelings seemed to have gained temporary control. My stomach grew ever more tense and nervous. I sometimes bit my lips to soreness. I often lost the power to concentrate on the work at hand. My resignation as prior brought no permanent solution. But it did bring relief which relaxed my defenses. The repressed emotions grabbed their opportunity and exploded in every direction. This period of life was a death for me. I could only hope for a resurrection.

I had never lost the conviction that healing was in process and that it was an inescapable task. Despite daily defeats there was hope of ultimate victory and freedom. The forward crawl into an honest confrontation with self continued. I had a choice to make, one between life and death. I had chosen life, which I could find only by entering death. The paschal mystery, the exodus journey, had to be enacted on the level of my inner psyche.

This forced exodus journey of 1965 was the gift of my own unconscious to my person. That same year I began what has become my major apostolic endeavor: retreats for couples, widows and widowers, and divorcees at our Family Life Center. My interior journey became easier as I met people hungry for the Lord. Through sharing the bread of the Lord's Word with them I myself was nourished and strengthened. The Scriptures became my viaticum along the way to fuller life. However, by 1969 I still was only crawling. A new meaning had come into my life through the retreat apostolate.

But I still experienced an "uprootedness" in having to release goals and dreams regarding my monastic community. For two years I lived outside the monastery while attending St. Louis University. I returned only on weekends to help with retreats. There was a release and safety in this distance from the abbey. But the hostile feelings still surged frequently out of control. I was still disturbed by my relationships with others. My being cried out for acceptance and appreciation, yet I lived in such a way that I did not call them forth. I was unable, as yet, joyfully to be the servant of all.

I did know with certainty, however, that something had begun to take place during this four-year crawl. There was a "movement" of forces in my psyche. I sensed a deep inner transformation establishing control over the unsurfaced emotions. I felt the beginning of a new wholeness.

With this growth came new insights regarding past behavior. I saw the extent to which my behavior was determined by my unconscious needs and impulses. I began to question the motives behind my struggles to keep an infant Pius X Monastery alive and growing. What had seemed to be obedience to God's Will or dedication to a monastic ideal could have been motivated by fears of failure and a quest for recognition. Such insights brought a deepening sense of gratitude to the Lord. I began to understand His loving fidelity toward me. How compassionate He had been with my weaknesses and ignorance! Truly He was a GOD-WITH-ME! Only later did I learn that this was His name, for He is indeed God-with-us!

My goal of rebirth was still unrealized in 1969. I was still in bondage, the victim of unconscious energies seeking the peace of integration. I longed to be outgoing, joyful, and compassionate. Father Prior assured me that my interior hostilities were not as evident to others as I feared. Though many thought I was a peace-loving monk who preached charity, love, and unity from the housetops, I knew myself to be aggressive and even belligerent. I wondered if my goal of rebirth was realistic. I wondered how much longer I could wait for it to become reality. The Lord, God-with-me, knew the thoughts of my heart. He answered my prayer.

It was the third weekend of January 1969. That Saturday night I had the opportunity to go to my first prayer meeting at Visitation Academy in St. Louis. Ordinarily I would have by-passed such an opportunity. But I was in need of special help. Weeks earlier I learned about developments brewing in my community that were deeply disturbing to me. They opened many of the past wounds that had led to my own resignation as prior five years earlier. The prayer meeting was a good experience. I discovered that people were *praying* what I had so often merely *talked about:* the love of the Father, the centrality of Jesus in the Christian life, the power of the Spirit. These were not merely intellectual truths but experienced realities. I saw people deeply touched by the God in whom they believed. I saw people not merely saying prayers but in deep communion with God. I liked what I saw. I wanted to return.

Since retreat work occupied my Saturday nights, I could not return to Visitation. I found a small ecumenical prayer group which met in a private home. During the two months that I prayed with this group I got the courage several times to ask for prayers. What I sought was the strength to live through the developments in my community. The strength came in the form of the Spirit as power. The gift of praying in tongues also came at this time. At first it was merely a flutter of my vocal cords: another example of how gently and unemotionally the Lord deals with me!

The power that came through these prayer meetings inspired a new dedication in me to the basic elements of monastic spirituality: the study and reading of Scripture, the presence of Jesus, and the power of the Spirit. The Lord began to reveal Himself to me through Scripture. This ongoing knowledge anchored me emotionally and intellectually as nothing else could. My monastic life took on a new meaning. The charismatic renewal was but a contemporary expression of the monastic renewal of the fourth, fifth, and sixth centuries. Through my initial contacts with the charismatic renewal it seemed the Lord was calling me to a new life and a new mission as a monk. I did not fully know this, however, until much later.

A new prior for my community was appointed in March 1969. The Lord blessed me by giving me a new trust in Him and His promises. I settled down to a full load of retreats. In early summer I gave a retreat to sisters wherein I asked Jesus to be the retreat master. I was astonished at what He did when I stayed out of His way.

Some weeks later I was sharing the pain of my life story with one of the retreatants, who was soon to leave as a missionary to Bolivia. I was standing near the window looking out when it happened. It happened before I was aware of it. I looked back into the room and said to my friend, "It is gone! The pain has left." This was the first of many healing graces the Lord had in store for me. For about two weeks I lived as a freed person. I assumed I was totally healed! How ignorant I was of the Lord's ways! What a disappointment to have much of the pain and anguish return! Yet all this was different. I had experienced wholeness; to be alive had been a deep joy. The experience strengthened my faith by confirming me in hope. Never again was the future to be as bleak as it had been.

This minimal contact with the charismatic renewal during the early months of 1969 had led me down a new road. It carried forward what the techniques of Jungian psychology had begun four years earlier. A transition was in progress. Today I still ponder the awesomeness of where this transition led me. The year 1970 became the most eventful of my life. That year I discovered the power of faith in Jesus and prayer to Him as the Lord of my life. That year I began my journey of surrender to the gift of Jesus as Lord, the gift of His Spirit.

Through the unexpected cancellation of a weekend retreat in January of that year I was able to take a few days' vacation with friends in Tulsa. During prayer the first morning I asked the Lord to show me the best way to spend the weekend. The answer flashed into my mind with jet speed: "Relax completely in the present moment. Be open to whatever My Spirit has in store for you in the present moment. Give no concern to the moment that has passed; have no concern for the moment that has not yet come."

In this spirit I began my vacation. Saturday I leisurely read material in preparation for a series of family retreats the following summer. That evening some members of the religious community joined me to plan the retreat I was to give them in June. Afterwards I found myself sharing with one of my friends my experience with the charismatic renewal. While sharing the story, I realized that that very weekend, the year before, I had attended my first prayer meeting.

During the night a sleet storm hit Tulsa. Travel was dangerous. Sunday was another leisurely, peaceful day. On Monday morning I was to visit with another friend. Upon my arrival, she told me the Lord had seemed to urge her all night long to take me to meet a certain Spirit-filled woman. Arrangements were made at once. Before the morning was over, we were at the woman's home.

Our initial conversation was brief. I told her of my contacts with the charismatic renewal. I spoke of the turmoil in my community. I assured her of my desire to know Jesus better. She suggested that we pray, the Lord wanted her to minister to me in His name. She stood beside me, imposed hands, and prayed in tongues. She spoke out in prophecy. Each word of the message resounded deeply in my spirit. I was awe-struck and dumb-founded. The message was so true. How could she know me that well? My whole life, it seemed to me, was laid out before me. Most surprising was that in every sentence of the message I heard echoes of the Lord's promise: "I will instruct you and teach you the way you should go; I will give you counsel with my eye upon you."

First, the Lord (for I really believe the Lord spoke through her as His prophet) revealed how much Satan had wanted to win me away from Christ. Satan had tried to do this through four evil spirits—those of depression, self-pity, rejection, and an excessive fear of other people's opinions. She asked me to proclaim Jesus as the Lord of my life. I thus acclaimed Christ's victory over all the forces of evil attacking me and professed belief in His sovereignty over the universe, especially over my life.

Then Jesus, through her prophetic words, assured me that He had always been my Lord, that He had kept me safe, and that He was now going to lead me into a new way of life. There should be no fear for He would be with me always. He would tell me all I needed to know. I was overwhelmed. The message was a restatement and promise of fulfillment of Psalm 32:8, the verse decorating my profession formula of twenty-nine years earlier!

Then she asked that the Lord grant me special gifts of His Spirit. She prayed for the gift of knowledge. She carefully explained that she was not asking for a natural wisdom but for knowledge given directly by the Spirit for understanding and proclaiming Jesus Christ as Lord of His people. She also prayed that I receive the gift of inner healing and a compassion for others in pain.

All this took place in about twenty minutes. I had a great desire to be alone with the Lord. The woman discerned what I was feeling and asked if I desired to leave. My friend and I bade her a quick farewell. We went back to my residence and relived the whole experience amidst tears of joy and wonderment over the goodness of the Lord. It was difficult later in the day to share the experience with the closest of my friends. Yet I had to bear witness to this wondrous deed of the Lord. I had to let others know that I had accepted the Lord's instructions and that I would take the road He would point out to me.

While sharing, I felt much like Abraham. I could identify with his call to walk with faith in the word the Lord spoke to him. I could identify with his vision of the future built only on the Lord's promises. I knew only through faith in the word I had heard that there was a promised land of freedom in store for me: freedom from depression, self-pity, fear of rejection, and fear of other people's opinions. The victory over these killing powers was not yet mine. But I could return to my monastery with new hope for victory born of a new-found faith. I had experienced the presence of the Spirit and the power of Jesus, my Lord. I returned to the monastery a different person.

Two days later I flew to Kansas City enroute to Emporia, Kansas, to fulfill a speaking engagement made months earlier. The Catholic parish in the town, pastored by Franciscan friars, was celebrating the Church Unity Octave. I had been asked to speak about the charismatic renewal in the Catholic Church. I tried to show the similarity between what was happening in the Catholic Church today and what had happened in the various "baptisms in the Spirit" recorded by Luke in Acts. I spoke for more than an hour and after a short break answered questions for two more hours. How hungry people were for the nourishment that comes only from the Word of God! I sensed how deep was their hope that what the Spirit was doing in the charismatic renewal would renew the whole Church.

The Lord did much for the people in Emporia that night. He did much more for me. I began to realize what it means to preach the Word "in the power of the Spirit." I had, of course, prepared for this lecture. But I used no notes, not even an outline. I spoke from the texts what the Spirit placed on my heart. New insights came as I was speaking. It was hard to believe I was saying what I heard myself saying. A new freedom had become mine. I already had confirmation regarding the "new way" of which the Lord had spoken the previous weekend in Tulsa.

I got to bed at 3:00 A.M. By 7:00 A.M. I was on my way to the airport to return home. I was scheduled to begin a retreat at Pevely that evening. Enroute to St. Louis, I was filled with praise and thanksgiving for all the Lord had done in just one week. I used the afternoon back at Pevely to prepare for the retreat. As the hours passed I became increasingly depressed. Fear gripped me. I had a great distaste for preaching this retreat. On my way to the retreat house that evening I stopped by the monastery chapel. I told the Lord He just had to be the retreat master; I was too empty and too tired. I hoped He could use me as His minister. This was another surrender in faith to the Lordship of Jesus. As I walked to the retreat house, I sensed keenly my own weakness and helplessness.

I have since called that retreat the first charismatic one held at Pevely. Neither my content nor my method was changed. Yet the whole retreat was different. I was different. A confrere working with me wondered what had happened, because what I was saying was so different. Most of the retreatants that weekend were physicians and professional people. They admitted they were shaken as never before. They had arrived complacent. One doctor wondered why he had come at all. He felt no need for a retreat that year. Yet he was the one most deeply touched. He realized his need for the Lord.

What hunger this group, too, showed for the Word and the Spirit! Several asked to be prayed over for the "baptism in the Spirit." I tried to put them off. I stated that they needed more preparation. This was indeed true. But the real reason for trying to procrastinate was my fear. I was only a neophyte "in the Spirit" myself. I had never prayed thus for others in public. Not all present were eager to move ahead in such "strange ways." (The following Monday my superior asked for an explanation of what had happened: He had heard by Sunday afternoon what a "strange" retreat this had been!) The retreatants, too, were afraid. Some had been jolted out of the complacency and security of a comfortable religion of minimum performance. Others sensed they were being called to commitment and surrender. They began to realize that faith in Jesus does not lead to complacency but to complete abandonment of one's life to His Lordship.

I wondered, too, where the Lord was leading me through this experience. I had in no sense "staged" the weekend or directed its course. I could only conclude that Jesus was teaching me more about His Lordship.

The preliminary journey of 1965–69 had been necessary before the Tulsa revelation of Jesus as Good Shepherd, as Lord of my life. But for the Tulsa event to become deeply rooted in my spirit, the summer of 1970 was necessary.

I was scheduled to lead seventeen retreats that summer, ranging in length from weekends to five or six full days, as well as two one-week workshops on prayer. Throughout that summer I usually returned to Pevely on a Friday afternoon for the weekend retreat and was off again to anywhere in the States by Sunday afternoon or evening. The schedule left me fearful. Did I have the physical and emotional stamina needed for such a workload? The morning I was to leave for the first retreat, the last week of May, I stayed in bed with a very bad cold. I wondered how I could go at all. While resting, waiting to be taken to the airport, I was thinking about the letter to the Ephesians, which I planned to use for this retreat. I began to sense that I should make a complete change in plans and use instead retreat material that was yet very much in the preparatory stage.

For three years I was a member of the renewal committee of the Benedictine Federation of the Americas. At the Federation's Renewal Chapter in October 1969 all of its renewal documents had been discussed, approved, and adopted. In March 1970 I had been asked to lead a retreat for the monks of one of the abbeys in the Federation and to base the content of the retreat on these renewal documents. I spent the following three months preparing for this retreat. I studied not only the renewal documents but the *Rule* of St. Benedict and Benedict's life by St.

Gregory the Great. Though in my earlier book[2] I sought to give a deeper understanding of the monastic way of life by Benedict, I now found something entirely new. I discovered Benedict's *faith* in Jesus. For Benedict, Jesus was truly Lord of the monastic community. The real purpose of his monastic way of life was to bring the monk and the monastic community to an acceptance of the power and love that Jesus as Lord has over all. I began to realize that Benedict's faith in Jesus was rooted in the scriptural witness. With these insights I now had the lead that was to guide me throughout the long series of summer retreats.

As I rested that morning the last week of May, I began to sense the possibility of not basing the upcoming retreat on Ephesians. But could the material on Benedict's way of life, ideal for Benedictines, be used for a community of religious women who were not Benedictine? Yet it seemed that this is what the Lord wanted. He wanted the theme of His Lordship to be brought to the sisters. I stepped out in faith. Before leaving the monastery, I had made the decision. This meant much extra work. I still did not have even rough outlines for the conferences of this new retreat. As the days of the retreat passed there was no doubt that the decision was the right one. The material answered the real needs of the sisters. It spoke directly to their situation. It even inspired them to action.

The climax came the last evening of the retreat. The teaching had been on the evil of murmuring. Murmuring was defined as the rejection of Jesus as Lord of a situation. I had recalled the Lord's response to His unhappy people in the desert:

> Now the people set up a lament which was offensive to Yahweh's ears, and Yahweh heard it. His anger blazed. . . . "you have rejected Yahweh who is with you, and have wailed before him saying: Why did we ever leave Egypt?" [Nb. 11:1, 20.][3]

[2] Wilfrid Tunink, O.S.B., *Vision of Peace* (New York: Farrar, Straus & Company, 1963).
[3] Except where otherwise indicated, all biblical quotations are taken from *The Jerusalem Bible* (Garden City, N.Y.: Doubleday & Company, Inc., 1966).

I ended with a strong exhortation that all accept Jesus as Lord and eliminate murmuring, rancor, and discontent from their lives.

There was little response by way of discussion. The group seemed unusually quiet. I had the feeling my message had been rejected. Then the superior of the house, as if moved by the same Spirit that led me to change the retreat material, invited all to come to the chapel that night. I went also. Everyone sat in the greatest silence for some time. Then the superior spoke again: "Let's all gather around the altar." They formed circles three deep in the sanctuary. Their heads were lowered in what seemed to be both shame and repentance. Soon they were confessing their sins to one another.

The next day I learned the background of this communal repentance. At this mother house were various categories of sisters, each with varying needs and interests. There were the candidates, postulants, and novices. The simply professed, still in training, were pursuing their education at local universities. There was the provincial staff and also those who ministered to the upkeep of the house. In the infirmary were the retired and the ill. There were many groups but there was no unity. There was division among the various groups. There was disunity among the members of each group. My message had touched the underlying cause of the disunity: the rampant spirit of murmuring. This is what the sisters confessed to each other. What a moving experience! The Lord was touching hearts as I stood there in their midst. I knew once again, through experience, that Jesus truly is Lord! He is alive. He is present. He is powerfully at work. I marveled at His wisdom and goodness in having the retreat material changed at the very last moment. I knew Him again as Lord faithful to His promised word: "I will instruct you and teach you the way you should go."

Frequently during that summer Jesus used such incidents to increase my faith in His Lordship. I learned much. It is impossible to box in the Spirit of Jesus. He seemed to work when and where one least expected to find Him. He always did the surprising, the unexpected thing. His obviously was a superior knowledge. He had His own plan, which He could carry out when He found a heart open to Him in faith. He did mighty and wonderful things. Always He acted in great gentleness. He answered real needs for real people. All He did revealed Him as Savior and Lord. All He did inspired a greater surrender to His Lordship.

And there was more I learned about His Lordship. What I had discovered while preparing the retreat during the spring months became anchored in the depths of my being during the summer months. While crisscrossing the country for the various retreats, I discovered an intimate bond between authentic monastic spirituality and the contemporary charismatic renewal. All summer I taught the scriptural background for the mystery of the Lordship of Jesus. All summer I reflected with my retreatants on the action of His Spirit, first in the life of Jesus and then in the life of the Christian. I grew in my understanding of the message as I moved from one group to another. The content of my teachings changed as my understanding grew. I began to find the message all through Scripture. I began to collect texts and incidents illustrating various aspects of the mystery. Never before had I been able to speak with such power and conviction out of the Word. The message touched me as well as the retreatants. I was called to greater faith and more fervent prayer. The message kept calling for an ever greater conversion of life and change of heart.

As the heavy summer schedule ended, I realized I was much improved physically, emotionally, and especially spiritually. What a special gift of Jesus this was! What a source of life and strength for the body as well as for the spirit of man this "other Advocate" could be! I knew my life was now set in a new direction. I had a new mission. My only aim was to live for Jesus as the Lord of my life.

The continuing daily search of the Scriptures revealed added insights. I began to understand that the Lordship of Jesus was the central tenet of the faith of the first Christians. "Jesus is

Lord" (1 Co. 12:3)! This was their jubilant and triumphant profession of faith. I saw in the Old Testament, too, that God's central revelation was that He was Lord. The basic discovery of the Israelites, the people this Lord had chosen for His own, was that their Lord was God. In due time they realized that he was the only true God because there was no other God. This was the faith about which they sang:

> Come, ring out our joy to the Lord;
>     hail the rock who saves us.
> Let us come before him, giving thanks,
>     with songs let us hail the Lord.
> A mighty God is the Lord
>     a great king above all gods.
>     [Ps. 94(95):1-3, Grail Translation.]

During the summer of 1970 I had made the same discovery as did the Israelites of old. It was an exciting time for me! I experienced for the first time a personal faith, something much more than an intellectual assent to a system of dogmas and rules. I found God! I discovered that He was Lord, my Lord! Most of all, as Lord He was God-with-me! And this made the difference. I traced the history of the name for God: Yahweh, I Am, to Adonai, to Kyrios, to Lord. Every "I am with you" scriptural passage touched me deeply. I knew God was revealing Himself as directly and as personally to me as He had to Moses (Ex. 3:1-15), to Joshua (Jos. 1:1-9), to Isaiah (Is. 6:1-13), to Jeremiah (Jr. 1:4-10), to the exiles in Babylon (Is. 41:8-14; 43:1-5). I now had a conviction that it was this God who through His Spirit had prompted me to place that eighth verse of Psalm 32 on my profession formula. It was indeed God, my Lord, instructing me and teaching me and giving me counsel, always keeping His eye upon me!

I now had the message I wanted to share with the married couples who came to the abbey for retreat. For the next three years the retreat content in some way centered on the themes of the Lordship of God and its full revelation in the Lordship of Jesus. I had known Jesus through the *Baltimore Catechism* and in the theology textbooks of the 1930s and 1940s as true God and true man. But the Jesus I now discovered was different. Yes, He was true God; He was also true man. But He was God and man now in ways that often boggled my mind. I could identify with Paul as he wrote to the Ephesians:

> You have probably heard how I have been entrusted by God with the grace he meant for you, and that it was by a revelation that I was given the knowledge of the mystery, as I have just described it very shortly. If you read my words, you will have some idea of the depths that I see in the mystery of Christ. [3:2-4.]

I saw depths in the mystery of Jesus which I had never suspected were there. They did not come to me by way of that kind of revelation of which I think St. Paul is speaking: the revelation he had on the road to Damascus, revelations which he continued to receive as he was present to the Lord in prayer. My insights into the mystery of Jesus came in a very normal way. They came as I continued to search the Scriptures, especially the New Testament. They came through the mutual sharing with couples weekend after weekend as we discerned what the chosen Scripture texts were saying about Jesus. They came as I saw couples through such sharing of the Word find Jesus and come to a vibrant faith in Him. They came as I heard these simple, often theologically uneducated people ask the most penetrating questions about Jesus, questions to which the Spirit gave the answers as we continued to share and pray.

What we learned about Jesus was always reducible to the action of the Spirit of Yahweh upon Him. This is how the New Testament Scriptures presented Jesus. He was a man conceived by Mary under the overshadowing power of the Spirit of God, a man who grew up guided by that Spirit. He was a man who received from His Father that Spirit in messianic fullness before He began His life's mission. He was a man who lived in the power and the wisdom of that Spirit, and died in His power. He rose from the dead to become, through that same Spirit, Lord! He was always divine. Only after He became Lord through His Resurrection was He known to be God the Father's only Son. In the power of the Spirit he returned to the Father so that in the Father's name He could give us the great gift the Father had so graciously and generously given Him, the gift of the Spirit.

These are some of the depths of knowledge and wisdom that I discovered in Jesus during those years of exciting retreat work with married couples. In the eight chapters which follow I share more of what the Lord Jesus taught us in our mutual search of Him. Each chapter represents a different stage in my journey into the mystery of Jesus. Each chapter represents an aspect of the mystery of the Lordship of Jesus which the Spirit revealed to me in these recent years. To me my journey seems very similar to that of the early disciples of Jesus, especially of the Jewish converts. They *started* their journey by coming to believe in the Lordship of God. From this foundation they went on to faith that Jesus was truly the Anointed One of their Lord; He was the Christ of God. They found it hard to accept Him as the Christ or the Messiah, for He was so much like other men! He was really a man like them in all things! Jesus spent His public ministry bringing His followers to believe that He was the Christ, not according to popular Jewish expectations but according to Yahweh's plan as recorded in His Word. Only after the Spirit came on Pentecost did they finally realize He was Lord and indeed the Son of God. Once they knew Him to be divine, they understood in a new way the other aspects of the mystery of His person.

This book is intended to describe stages that could be a journey for you also. I suggest a quick reading of the entire book and then a careful study, letting each chapter be a guide for your personal journey into a new faith in Jesus.

There is no end to this journey. My own journey into a living experience of Jesus as Lord has not ended. In the summer of 1974 I researched the Gospel of John. I have absorbed only a small portion of its riches, but one thing I know. The Jesus I have come to experience is the Jesus John presents in his Gospel! I would never have known Jesus as given by John had I not first made that journey of faith.

I hope that the Spirit who bore witness to me that God is Lord and Father, and that Jesus is Christ and Lord, will in some way through these words sound the same message in the depths of your own spirit.

## A Final Comment

I am aware of the many questions raised by scholars in their exegesis of the Old Testament, particularly in relationship to the Pentateuch. These questions and critical discussions have shed much light on the historicity of the background, the events, and the personages of the Bible, as well as on the manner of composition of the received texts as we now have them. I am not ignoring such findings and conclusions. In many ways I rely heavily upon modern exegesis. I am, however, taking a different approach in my presentation of Moses, for example, and his message. It is an approach that seeks the spiritual message of the Scriptures not apart from but within the literal meaning of the Word of the Lord as we have received it. This message is above all contained in the word that is God's name. The name of God, Yahweh, and the message it contains in itself, is in turn the key to understanding the rest of Scripture.

# CHAPTER I

# I Shall Be with You

I once received a letter so full of joy and hope that it changed my life. The message of that letter had a power over me, lifting me and making me joyful in spirit.

It is my hope that the message I am bringing you through this book will have a similar effect upon you. I hope it will influence your life as it has mine.

The message I bring you was first heard nearly four thousand years ago. It is an old and ancient message. But there is always something new and fresh about it. It has been tested by centuries of experience. It is more relevant today than ever before. Its full meaning and its implications for human life have scarcely been tapped.

This message did not come from the heart of man. It was spoken by man to man, yes; but it came right out of the heart of God. It is a message that contains in itself all the words God ever spoke to man. It is a message that is but a word, the word in which God revealed Himself to mankind. That word is God's proper name.

## A Name—What Is There in a Name?

Do you realize what your name means to you, or what your name might mean to other people? Think of that person in the whole world who means most to you. Can you think of that person without thinking of his or her name?

A child even before birth is thought of in terms of a name. As its parents search for a name for this unborn child, his or her identity begins to emerge. Through the use of that name later the child's identity is confirmed. So, too, when people meet they begin to discover each other through the use of their names.

Recently I was talking with a person who was trying to understand why she was nameless on her birth certificate. She was described merely as "the fourth child" of her parents. Years later, though convinced of the lifelong love of her parents for her, she wondered why her life had begun in such anonymity. She found it disturbing to know she had been nameless even for a short time. As a result, she wondered about her true identity.

Helen Keller, in the story of her life, gives a gripping account of her realization "that everything and everyone has a name." Being blind, she had to *touch* every person and everything to learn what they had to say to her. In discovering the name of the person and thing touched, she in turn *was touched*. She became herself. She realized her identity by each new identifying experience.

It should not be hard for us, therefore, to understand why ancient peoples gave such importance to the choice of names. For them the naming of a child was a serious responsibility. The name could not be just any name. It had to fit; it had to be a name that expressed the character of the child and the uniqueness of its life. The name had to express those traits that it was hoped would emerge as the infant grew up. For ancient peoples the name captured both the essence and the destiny of the person. The name was the life of its owner; hence, it was not to be given or taken away.

These facts help us understand why the Israelites of old gave such importance to God's revelation of Himself under His proper name.

## Tell Me Your Name

The patriarch Jacob on one occasion had pleaded with God: "I beg you, tell me your name" (Gn. 32:30). We sense from this appeal that there is no way man can know God unless he knows His name. But our God is a great God. He is so great He has many names. Each name reveals something new and different about Him. But there is one name which is special. It is what God calls His proper name. It is the name which, more than any other, reveals who God really is. Once God had revealed Himself under this name, there was nothing more for Him to say. He had said it all.

God did not use this name when He first began speaking to man. He did not use it when He spoke to Abraham, Isaac, or Jacob. There must have been a good reason why God did not reveal who He really was to these patriarchs. When Jacob cried out, "Tell me your name," God did not give His proper name even then. Why? We can only guess. Maybe Jacob would not have understood the name. Maybe he would have found it difficult to accept what God was saying about Himself in using His proper name. God's use of His proper name would have demanded such a drastic departure from man's usual way of thinking about God that man would have found it difficult to accept a god with such a name. There is a passage in Exodus that leads us to suppose something like this would have happened had God revealed His name sooner:

> God spoke to Moses and said to him, ". . . To Abraham and Isaac and Jacob I appeared as El Shaddai; I did not make myself known to them by my name. . . ." [6:2–3.]

To the patriarchs God was El Shaddai. This was language they could understand. They could accept an El Shaddai god.

Such a god was like the other gods in whom they had believed and in whom other men still believed. For *El Shaddai* means "god of the mountaintops." This God who called Himself El Shaddai was, in effect, saying, "I am as mysterious and distant, as aloof and inaccessible, as mighty and majestic as the mountaintops." All peoples believed this about their gods. They were wholly "other," different from everything they could see and touch. Their gods were far away, distant, untouchable.

The God who spoke to the patriarchs did not completely break with this manner of thinking and speaking about Himself. The patriarchs had known only an El Shaddai god. They used very earthy images to give expression to this "otherness" of God. To them God was like the mountain, far away, unconcerned, majestic, inapproachable.

## I Am Yahweh

But God wanted to say more to Moses than He had said to the patriarchs:

> God spoke to Moses and said to him, "*I am Yahweh*. To Abraham and Isaac and Jacob I appeared as El Shaddai; I did not make myself known to them by *my name Yahweh*." [Ex. 6:2–3, italics added.]

What does God's real name of Yahweh mean? What kind of god can call Himself Yahweh? What did He need of His creatures before He could reveal Himself to them as Yahweh? The answers to these questions are given in the story of Moses.

Moses had known God as El Shaddai, for we must assume that Abraham and the other patriarchs had passed on to their descendants their experiences of God as El Shaddai. Stories about the God who spoke to them had become an oral tradition. Such stories had often been told in religious services or in the intimacy of the family circle. Surely Moses knew these stories and kept them in his heart. Surely he knew and accepted El Shaddai as his God.

But the life of Moses had been unique, even tragic. He had experienced emptiness, loneliness. He was hungry for more than life had yet offered. His tragic life had opened him up. It had made him ready for a new and different relationship with God. Moses may not have been looking for a different kind of God consciously. But he was willing, even eager, to accept a God who was not so distant, aloof, or inaccessible as El Shaddai. He was ready for Yahweh, a God who truly would be with him.

We know the basic facts of the life of Moses. Let us put ourselves into his shoes to understand better why God was now free to say to Moses what He could not say to the patriarchs.

The parents of Moses belonged to the tribe of Levi. They believed in El Shaddai and were loyal to Him. When other tribes apostatized, these Levites remained faithful. The parents of Moses showed fidelity to their God by the way they endured the circumstances surrounding their son's birth. They sensed the power of El Shaddai's protection after Moses was born. Cautiously they hid Moses and squelched his every cry for fear that Pharaoh's soldiers would find him and murder him. Finally after three long, fear-filled months, they knew they could conceal their son no longer. So they set him adrift in a basket made of reeds near a place where Pharaoh's daughter was bathing in the river. She was moved with pity for him and rescued the child. She gave him to a Hebrew girl, the sister of Moses, who just happened to be nearby! She in turn gave the child to his own mother to be nursed and reared. When Moses grew up, his mother, according to agreement, brought him to Pharaoh's daughter, who "treated him like a son" (Ex. 2:10). There in the royal palace Moses grew up, amidst its luxury and its court etiquette. He was taught all the wisdom of the Egyptians. This poor Hebrew boy, who should have been killed at birth according to Pharaoh's edict, grew up in the very presence of the Pharaoh!

But a day came when all this changed. The Scriptures tell us how it happened:

> Moses, a man by now, set out at this time to visit his countrymen, and he saw what a hard life they were having; and he saw an

Egyptian strike a Hebrew, one of his countrymen. Looking around he could see no one in sight, so he killed the Egyptian and hid him in the sand. On the following day he came back, and there were two Hebrews, fighting. He said to the man who was in the wrong, "What do you mean hitting your fellow countryman?" "And who appointed you," the man retorted, "to be prince over us, and judge? Do you intend to kill me as you killed the Egyptian?" [Ex. 2:11–14a.]

The Scriptures are equally descriptive of what followed:

Moses was frightened. "Clearly that business has come to light," he thought. When Pharaoh heard of the matter he would have killed Moses, but Moses fled from Pharaoh and made for the land of Midian. And he sat down beside a well. [2:14b–15.]

We can imagine what the thoughts of Moses were as he sat there dejectedly by the well. Life had changed very suddenly and drastically for him. He had had to leave Egypt very abruptly and had escaped to this land of Midian because he was a murderer. In the months that followed he became Jethro's son-in-law and tended his flocks. Moses must have anguished many times over his plight: from the royal palace of Pharaoh to the lonely life of a herdsman on the hot desert plains and hillsides of the Sinai peninsula. What an unexpected trip Moses had taken! And things didn't improve much for him for seven long years!

Moses had many hours to ponder his changed circumstances: this murderer, this exiled refugee, this shepherd who was once a courtier in the palace of Pharaoh. He had been near the top of the social ladder; now he was at the bottom. But he was at the very place God is wont to find man, the place where man is open to God.

Moses was looking after the flock of Jethro. . . . He led his flock to the far side of the wilderness and came to Horeb, the mountain of God. [Ex. 3:1.]

As Moses sat there, drearily and dreamily watching his flock, God broke into his life. God confronted him with the full reality of His divine being, and with the fact that He was the God bearing the unique name of Yahweh!

## The Blazing Bush

There the angel of Yahweh appeared to him in the shape of a flame of fire, coming from the middle of a bush. Moses looked; there was the bush blazing but it was not being burned up. "I must go and look at this strange sight," Moses said, "and see why the bush is not burned." [Ex. 3:2–3.]

We could be sidetracked by the various interpretations of this burning bush. Some see it as sheer nonsense; others look on it as a miracle. Some argue it was a bush actually burning yet not being burned up. Others argue this was a divinely inspired but imaginary scene.

Such argumentation misses the point of the story: This was God's way of getting Moses to pay attention to Him! This was Yahweh's way of breaking unmistakably into the life experience of Moses. And God broke in with such force that never again could Moses deny the reality of what he had experienced or the truth of what he had been told. The burning bush represents the merciful love of a God speaking to Moses and revealing Himself as Yahweh. It depicts what is so often lacking in the lives of people: an initial life-changing encounter with God. Only on such an encounter can a life of faith in Him and of humble, loving service to man be built.

The necessity of such a "burning bush" cannot be denied. Every saint, religious founder, and leader has had one. Every such person can look back on some experience and say, "That's where I met God!" Because they really met God, their lives changed and continued to change. They became truly religious people, bound to God through the impact of that first encounter with Him.

Because God is Yahweh, a God with us, we can experience the living God. Anyone who believes God is Yahweh needs a Moses-like openness to God. Only because God is Yahweh can a life-changing encounter with Him take place. Only then does one know God to be truly present. The mystery and tragedy of the

Old Testament story is that the people refused to let Yahweh be Yahweh, God with them. They believed Him to be Yahweh, but never really surrendered themselves to Him. They did not have the humble, open faith of Moses. Though Yahweh revealed Himself to them, their lives showed they did not really believe in this kind of God. They paid Him only lip service.

Scripture often complains about people unable to let Yahweh into their lives, people who refused a real encounter with the living God, people of little faith. This happened, for example, when Moses was away for a short while:

> When the people saw that Moses was a long time coming down from the mountain, they gathered round Aaron and said to him, "Come, make us a god to go at the head of us; this Moses, the man who brought us up from Egypt, we do not know what has become of him." Aaron answered them, "Take the gold rings out of the ears of your wives and your sons and daughters, and bring them to me." So they all took the gold rings from their ears and brought them to Aaron. He took them from their hands and, in a mold, melted the metal down and cast an effigy of a calf. "Here is your God, Israel," they cried, "who brought you out of the land of Egypt!" . . . And so, early the next day they offered holocausts and brought communion sacrifices. [Ex. 32:1–6.]

How easily Israel apostatized in her faith-emptiness! Her promises to Yahweh were as yet mere lip service.

In Judges 2:16–19, we again see a people without the experience of a genuine God-encounter:

> Then Yahweh appointed judges for them, and rescued the men of Israel from the hands of their plunderers. But they would not listen to their judges. They prostituted themselves to other gods, and bowed down before these. Very quickly they left the path their ancestors had trodden in obedience to the orders of Yahweh. . . . They followed other gods; they served them and bowed before them, and would not give up the practices and stubborn ways of their ancestors at all.

These people were unable to persevere in their conversion to Yahweh. Their initial faith in Him died as they turned to false

gods. How headstrong and idolatrous they became as they shut
Yahweh out of their lives!

Through the prophet Samuel, God called Saul to save and lead
the people. But Saul did not remain open to the power of the
God he had experienced earlier. So the human struggle and a
jealousy as hard as hell flamed up in him:

> As David was returning after killing the Philistine, the women
> came out to meet King Saul from all the towns of Israel, singing
> and dancing to the sound of tambourine and lyre and cries of joy;
> and as they danced the women sang:
>
> > "Saul has killed his thousands,
> > and David his tens of thousands."
>
> Saul was very angry. . . . And Saul turned a jealous eye on
> David from that day forward. [1 S. 18:6–9.]

Who of us has not been an Israel or a Saul? Have we not our
false gods? Do we not seek our own praise? Are we not jealous?
Our faith, too, is often merely lip service, for we are not open to
that life-changing encounter which Yahweh has waiting for us.

We too need a "burning bush" to come to know God as He really is. We need that burning bush again and again! If you yet
insist that burning bushes are useless, I ask: Why then is our
faith in God so weak? Why don't we know God as He really is?
Why do fear and worry strangle our freedom to trust Him? Most
of all, why are we too busy to commune with God? The living
God is waiting to manifest Himself to us initially, and again and
again. That is what the burning bush was for Moses. That is
what it is for us as we come to know God as He really is.

## Take Off Your Shoes

Once God had broken into Moses' life, he had to respond.
Moses could have walked away because of fright, a lack of interest, or the pressure of other concerns. But he was down and out.
He needed help; he was desperate. So he was ready to move forward. He was now an emptied self. How he thirsted for an

infilling! Moses, the disconsolate one, was about to become Moses, the radiant one. Moses, the murderer, was not only to be freed from personal guilt but was to deliver all of Israel. ". . . they put their faith in Yahweh and in Moses, his servant" (Ex. 14:31).

We have seen how God first spoke His Yahweh revelation to Moses. Moses was ready for this revelation and ready to experience its meaning through his burning bush. He was ready to meet his new God, to be changed, to accept the ensuing involvement. Scripture describes the response of Moses. God had used the strange sight of the burning bush to get Moses to pay attention to Him. But now a strange phenomenon is recorded. As Moses starts walking toward God, God suddenly stops him in his tracks and forbids him to come forward:

> Now Yahweh saw him go forward to look, and God called to him from the middle of the bush. "Moses, Moses!" he said. "Here I am," he answered. "Come no nearer," he said. "Take off your shoes, for the place on which you stand is holy ground." [Ex. 3:4–5.]

I often wondered why God demanded that Moses take off his shoes before stepping forward. This seems to be a meaningless demand. But one day I found the answer in the following passage in the Book of Ruth:

> Now in former times it was the custom in Israel, in matters of redemption or exchange, to confirm the transaction by one of the parties removing his sandal and giving it to the other. In Israel this was the form of ratification in the presence of witnesses.

And a footnote on this passage from Ruth in the Jerusalem Bible reads:

> To put one's foot on a field, or to throw a sandal on to it is to take possession of it. . . . The sandal thus becomes the symbol of the right of ownership. By taking it off and handing it to the purchaser the owner transfers the right to him. [Rt. 4:8, note c.]

So we have the key to an understanding of why God commanded Moses to take off his shoes before coming any closer to

Him in the burning bush. To truly meet Yahweh, Moses *had* to leave behind *all* his possessions. God was telling Moses, "You cannot come to Me in a living encounter and I cannot be for you the God, Yahweh, I wish to be unless you leave behind all of your possessions. Moses, I want you to express your willingness to surrender all your possessions by removing your shoes before you come any closer."

We might retort that Moses had nothing but his shoes left! They were his only possession at the time. He had already exchanged a developed land for a desert, a royal palace for a nomad's tent, and witty court companions for dumb cattle and sheep. What more was there for him to relinquish?

There was much more. Moses still had dreams and ambitions. He had plans for returning someday to Egypt. These plans had been thought about, analyzed, and finally decided upon during the lonely hours of shepherding. Moses yet had his will, his very life. He still possessed himself. He remained his own boss. But God could not be Yahweh, a God with Moses, as long as Moses was his own lord and master.

This God revealing Himself to Moses is no ordinary God. He is unique by wishing to be God with His people. He begins to sensitize Moses to the meaning of having such a God. God cannot be Yahweh for Moses unless He is his Lord. "Come no nearer. . . . Take off your shoes, for the place on which you stand is holy ground." The ground is holy because it marks the spot where Moses was invited to enter the mystery of God as Yahweh.

This passage gives us a law of authentic encounter with God; it describes how we can come to union with Him. There can be no union with God while we continue to wear our own "shoes," even one of them. We cannot live with this God and say at the same time, "I will serve You, but I will do it by keeping my rights and privileges, my plans for the future. I will serve You, but I expect You to increase my possessions. I will serve You, but I will continue to be my own lord and master!"

Such qualified service might be possible for us if our God were El Shaddai, an aloof, unconcerned God. But this God is Yahweh.

He says very simply, "Take off your shoes; give up all your possessions; give up even yourself. Only then can I be Yahweh, God-with-you. Only then can you enter into a deep communion with Me."

As yet, Moses did not understand the implications of God calling Himself Yahweh. God had yet to tell Moses what He was like just because He was Yahweh. There was no better way for Him to do this than to let Moses know He had always been aware of the condition of His people in Egyptian slavery. So God began speaking to Moses about His relationship with his ancestors.

## The God of Your Fathers

"I am the God of your father," he said, "the God of Abraham, the God of Isaac and the God of Jacob." At this Moses covered his face, afraid to look at God. [Ex. 3:6.]

There is historical continuity in God's revelation of Himself as Yahweh. A God who is Yahweh is a God who is with every human being. So the God who is now speaking to Moses is the God who spoke to Abraham. For Moses to learn that the God now speaking to him was the same God who had spoken to Abraham and the patriarchs must have been reassuring. Moses knew how God had intervened in their lives. Yet that God was El Shaddai, the awesome one of majesty and power. There was the tradition that no one could see this God and live, for He was so august and mighty. Yet here was Moses looking at Him in the burning bush! The voice he was hearing was in that very bush! With quick instinct Moses was filled with fear that he would die. He "covered his face, afraid to look at God."

Yahweh understood the reaction of Moses. But He kept on talking. For now Moses was ready to hear more of what this God was like:

And Yahweh said, "I have seen the miserable state of my people in Egypt. I have heard their appeal to be free of their slave drivers. Yes, I am well aware of their sufferings. I mean to deliver

them out of the hands of the Egyptians and bring them up out of
that land to a land rich and broad, a land where milk and honey
flow. . . . And now the cry of the sons of Israel has come to me,
and I have witnessed the way in which the Egyptians oppress
them." [3:7–10a.]

Moses could scarcely believe what he was hearing! He had
hoped for a solution to his personal problem. But the God who is
talking to him knows not only his personal problem but the
problems of all his countrymen. This is not an abstract, imper-
sonal knowledge. It is an awareness that moves Him deeply. He
hears the people's cries. *He has His answer.* He will take them
out of Egypt and move them to another country. He will replace
their slavery with freedom, their starvation was sufficient food.

This is no disinterested God. This is a new God with a new
name. He knows everything. He has a heart. He hears and answers prayers. He has plans and the power to fulfill them. He is
concerned with individuals as well as with a whole nation. We
wonder what the thoughts of Moses were at this graced moment
of human history, this moment when God first revealed Himself
as Yahweh.

But then came the stunning announcement:

"So come, I send you to Pharaoh to bring the sons of Israel, my
people, out of Egypt." [3:10b.]

Moses surely did not expect this! He panicked. Nothing had
been said to prepare him for this. Moses felt he was not the man
for the job. Had he not escaped from a Pharaoh whose subject
he had murdered? True, another Pharaoh was now on the
throne, but Moses was still a hunted man. The present Pharaoh
was less favorably disposed toward the Hebrews than the former
one. He was mercilessly driving them to despair. Moses could expect no mercy from such a ruler:

Moses said to God, "Who am I to go to Pharaoh and bring the
sons of Israel out of Egypt?" [3:11.]

Moses was saying, "Obviously, Yahweh, You can't be serious
about sending me! I am not the man for the job. I cannot do
what You want me to do."

God's response came with stunning swiftness and reassuring firmness: "I SHALL BE WITH YOU."

"I shall be with you." No god had ever said that! But no other god was Yahweh! These words reveal why God is Yahweh. God was saying to Moses, "There is no reason for you to hesitate, no reason for you to be afraid to return to Egypt and enter the very confines of Pharaoh's court—because I shall be with you, by your side, in your mind, in your heart. Do not hesitate, Moses, for I will be your wisdom, strength, and protection. I am Yahweh. I am a God whose whole being calls for union with My people. I am a God who desires to share life. I am Yahweh, Moses. I will be with you as you carry out the mission I have given you."

God promises Moses a sign so he will know Yahweh has spoken all these words:

"And this is the sign by which you shall know that it is I who have sent you . . . After you have led the people out of Egypt, you are to offer worship to God on this mountain." [3:12.]

God is now declaring, "Moses, My being with you is a mystery of faith. You will have to believe that I shall be with you. You will have to put your trust in these words I speak, words which give you the meaning of My name. I am truly a God for My people only when I live with them. Moses, this trust in Me will not be blind. You will have evidence of My being with you. I shall be acting in you and through you. There shall be signs of My being with you as you lead My people from this land. The greatest sign will happen when you have completely fulfilled this mission: When My people arrive at this very spot where you are now standing, you will know that I have been with you. You will then know Me as Yahweh. Then you will know I am God always with you.

"So, Moses," God continues, "go back to Egypt to My people. Give them My real name as you tell them you are going to lead them out of Egypt because the 'God of their Fathers' sent you to them."

Yahweh has been God's name for all generations. It is His

name unto this very day. The historical continuity of God's revelation of Himself as Yahweh endures. The God who spoke to Abraham and to Moses and who revealed Himself in Jesus is the same God whom we call "Our Father."

As I began this chapter, I wrote of a message which brought me joy and hope, strength and comfort. I hope the message of this chapter has brought you a similar experience. For this is the message: Our God does not merely exist; He lives by being with us. His great glory and desire is to be with us. "This is my name for all time; by this name I shall be invoked for all generations to come" (Ex. 3:15b).

Mankind received this message long ago. Through the intervening ages Yahweh has proved His Word to be true. But we know the truth of His Word only when we personally experience Him as God-with-us. Moses had to walk *toward* his burning bush; he had to walk on *after* finding it. Each of us needs to journey *to* a burning bush wherein we find God as Yahweh. And then we need to journey on *from* that bush into a life where we find God as Yahweh, with us indeed. In finding Him we find ourselves and one another. In finding Him as Yahweh, we find Him who created us so that He can be with us always, not only in eternity but even now in this life. We must leave our shoes behind as we begin our journey, as we come to an ever new perception of the meaning of His name. We start the journey *not* by walking but by first *believing* that God has said to each of us, "I SHALL BE WITH YOU."

# CHAPTER II

# Courage:
# Do Not Be Afraid

Christianity is a revealed religion. This means that in its faith, its cult, and its morality it depends on what God says rather than on what man thinks. God, in revelation, can talk about many things. But the most important topic of revelation is God Himself. What God says about Himself is what ultimately determines the character of faith, the quality of cult, and the nature of religious morality.

Christianity is unique. This is because of what God has said about Himself. He is Yahweh, a God-with-us. This name expresses His inner life, His divine nature, and His relationship with us. We do not know God unless we know Him as God-with-us.

God first revealed Himself as Yahweh, Lord, God-with-us, to Moses. But God continues to reveal Himself as Yahweh. This revelation is His fundamental message to man in the Old Testament. This revelation is the foundation upon which the edifice of both the Old and New Testaments is built. Once we acknowledge that this revelation is central to the Old Testament and is fulfilled in the New, another fact follows. Everything about Jesus and Christianity must refer back to, and be understood in the light of, the mystery of God as Yahweh, or Lord.

## Yahweh–Kyrios–Lord

We have called God Yahweh. We have called Him Lord. We
have said He is God-with-us. What reason is there for these various titles? The answer lies in the history of biblical translations.
*Yahweh* is God's proper name in Hebrew. This is shown in the
modern Jerusalem Bible translation, which keeps *Yahweh* as the
divine name throughout the Old Testament. Most other translations into English use the term *Lord*. The ancient Hebrews in
time came to feel that the name of Yahweh was too holy to pro-
nounce, and so it became their custom to substitute the word
*Adonai*, meaning "Lord," when reading the Scriptures aloud.
When the Jewish Scriptures were translated into the Greek Sep-
tuagint, this was rendered by the Greek word *Kyrios*. Then when
the Greek Old Testament, via the Latin, was translated into English, *Kyrios* was translated as *Lord*.

From this summary of the linguistics of the word "Lord" we
learn two things: First, it is legitimate to call God our Lord and
imply that this is His proper name; and, secondly, our primary
understanding of "Lord" should not be in the light of its English
or Greek meanings. We must read into the English word "Lord"
the meaning intended by God when He revealed Himself under
His proper name of *Yahweh*.

Many people are uneasy with the Jerusalem Bible translation
because it retains the Hebrew form *Yahweh* for the divine name.
However, through this translation readers were reintroduced to
the original divine name. This challenges us, who call God
"Lord," to understand our profession of faith in terms of understanding the original Hebrew word. The better we understand
the Lordship of God from the Old Testament writings, the better
we will come to know the central belief of the Christian community, namely, that now Jesus is our Lord.

Precious, indeed, is this divine name. It is God's gift to us. We
can know the real God only if He speaks to us about Himself,

only if we believe what He says to us about Himself. It was a significant moment, indeed, in the history of mankind, in the history of Judaism and Christianity, when God revealed Himself to Moses.

By telling us His name, God gave us an understanding of what He is like. "God" is the name which all nations have given to their deities. But as a name it is too general. In the minds of people this title refers to a supreme being, to one who is the first and final cause, to one who is the ultimate arbiter and judge of mankind.

Throughout history nations have given specific names to their gods, names which they thought expressed what their gods were like. These names, however, did not reveal the real life of their gods any more than did the designation "god" itself. But the divine name which God gives Himself is different. It tells us who He really is and it becomes our way of growing in the knowledge of our God. As we come to understand the name *Yahweh* we come to know the God-who-is.

The divine name, *Yahweh,* through its Greek and English equivalents of *Kyrios* and *Lord,* does express the idea of superiority. It connotes power, for the *kyrios* in Greek culture was a person in authority. He wielded power and dominion. The English *lord* conveys the same meaning. And so Yahweh is a God of majesty and power, of authority and dominion.

But when God called Himself *Yahweh,* He wished to say more. He wanted us to know that though He had supreme authority and dominion over us, He was, nevertheless, with us. He is God and He remains God in being present with us. This is the heart of the message expressed in God's revelation of Himself as Yahweh. He is truly God and He remains God, but as God He takes up His dwelling in our midst. He is with us. He lives with us. He works for us. He is involved in our life. He challenges us. He commits Himself to our cause. He draws us in love to accept Him as Lord, as Yahweh.

Moses in his openness to this new revelation came to know what this God was really like. He had known God as El Shaddai.

He did not lose his faith in such a God. For it was the El Shaddai God who was now saying He was Yahweh.

A new life began to open up for him. Having heard that God was with him, Moses found out that God truly *was* with him. He found manifestations of God in his life never before experienced. Through these experiences of God present and active in his life he grew in faith. He had heard the God who said, "I am with you." Now he realized, as he reflected on his life experiences, that this was really true He could no longer explain his thinking, his words, his actions, in terms of his own abilities. He was acting, but someone else was acting through him. His experiences strengthened his faith. In turn, he was brought to a greater acceptance of the mystery of God as Yahweh as he fulfilled his life's mission. Because of the faith-openness of Moses to God, God could more completely be a God-with-him. God was freer to move in and through Moses in the accomplishment of the mission for which He had chosen him. So Moses was continually learning more of what God, Yahweh, was like.

In the burning bush God revealed to Moses something about the quality of His divine life and something about His purpose in revelation. He did not choose Moses for a mission and then send him forth alone to fulfill it. He remained with Moses all the time he was fulfilling his mission. Moses experienced God's presence and came to believe in it with ever greater conviction. Through this faith and these continuing experiences Moses came to know God Himself. He was convinced God was with him. He grew in the trust that God would never desert him; that He was always by his side.

In light of this we can understand the so-called "ten plagues" of Egypt. They were truly plagues for Pharaoh and the Egyptians. For them they were grave disasters. But for Moses they were experiences of God's fidelity to His name and to His inner nature.

Through this repeated experience of God working through him in situations of difficulty Moses came into a firm faith that his God was indeed Yahweh. These ten plagues were the training period in which God confirmed Moses in the faith He demanded of him. Without these experiences of God-being-with-him, Moses would not have trusted his God later when the Israelites panicked before the approaching might of the Egyptian army. That incident is vividly described in the Book of Exodus:

> As Pharaoh approached, the sons of Israel looked around—and there were the Egyptians in pursuit of them! The sons of Israel were terrified and cried out to Yahweh. To Moses they said, "Were there no graves in Egypt that you must lead us out to die in the wilderness? What good have you done us, bringing us out of Egypt? We spoke of this in Egypt, did we not? Leave us alone, we said, we would rather work for the Egyptians! Better to work for the Egyptians than die in the wilderness!" Moses answered the people, "Have no fear! Stand firm, and you will see what Yahweh will do to save you today: the Egyptians you see today, you will never see again. Yahweh will do the fighting for you: you have only to keep still." [14:10–14.]

Moses did not have the faith he exemplified on this occasion when he began his mission. But God had been with him as He promised. Moses had learned he could trust his God and believe His word. God had trained him in faith. He had strengthened him through many confrontations. Moses was reborn by his trust in the God whose name was Yahweh. Now he was sure Yahweh would come to his aid. He stood there at the Sea of Reeds facing the panicking Israelites as the Egyptian cavalry galloped toward them. With calm conviction Moses told the sons of Israel not to be afraid of the advancing Egyptians, for Yahweh would deal with them. And Yahweh did!

It is not hard for us to identify with the Israelites. We have been in similar situations of fright and tension. Fear has gripped us too. We read of robberies and murders in the newspapers, and we sense that we could have been the victims. In such a crisis would we have had the faith of Moses? Or would we have buckled beneath the fear? Moses had learned to trust Yahweh's word. He was free from all fear and anxiety. His trust was perfected through many faith-testings. Though God is with us, He continues to test our faith. He does not prevent situations that cause fear and anxiety. But He does sustain us amid that fear and anxiety.

God's I-am-with-you promise did not end with Moses. If it had, we could not get excited about the Yahweh-revelation. What makes the name Yahweh, Lord, such good news is that God makes the same promise to us. The good news is that God wishes to be with all His people. He was with the Israelites throughout the whole of their history. He was with Jesus, His Incarnate Son, during His earthly existence. He has been with Christians through the ages. He is with you and me. To all of us He is constantly saying, "Do not be afraid, for I am with you."

## The Only Thing God Has to Say

Why did God repeat this revelation so often? Wouldn't it have been sufficient to give this astounding word to Moses alone?

There are many reasons why God has told us so often that He is with us. Two reasons have been meaningful to me. The first refers to God Himself. If God is Yahweh, if He is a God who is always with us, if this is His name, His inner life, then why should He not assure us over and over that He is with us? If God in His inner being is to be a God-with-us, what else can He really say to us? What else does He really want us to hear? Would it not be His one desire for us to know Him as He is, for what He is? Would He not betray His own nature if He did not reveal Himself as Yahweh to every generation and to every individual? Must He not continually repeat the deepest desire of His heart for us: "I am Yahweh; I am a God who is always with you"?

If we remember the incisive phrase of St. John, "God is love," we can speak of a divine psychology. Do lovers ever tire of telling each other about their love? If they do tire or do not speak of their love, is this not a sign that the relationship has begun to weaken? We need to be told, to be assured over and over that we are loved. There is no other way for human beings to build up true community. Community is the common unity of persons who affirm each other through loving and appreciative acceptance.

This is what God does by constantly revealing Himself to us. God is busy building community, that community lost by sin. God is at work reassuring us, inviting us to abandon our life of alienation from others. He draws us together with Him in sacred covenant. He loves us even when we don't love Him. God's love is real love. He says this in His way, a way that assures us: "I love you so much that I will take up My dwelling with you; I will be with you; I will never abandon you, never desert you." God is love and so He is in love with us. He has to keep on telling us He will remain with us.

## So Hard to Believe

The second reason why God says so often that He is with us concerns man. It is not easy to believe God is Yahweh. We find it hard to believe that God wants to be so close as to be always with us. We know how hard it is to believe people when they assure us they will be with us and will support us. We have been hurt so often that faith in other people does not come easily. It is hard to accept their expressions of trust. In a similar way faith in God does not come easily.

In our personal relationship with Him in the past we did not experience Him as a God of love and wisdom. We tried to serve Him and seemingly were let down. How often we were taught about the anger and wrath of God! We learned to expect punishment from Him. The emphasis placed on the transcendence of God seemed to bar us from Him. We were told He was far from us and we concluded He was far away. How easy to believe God is distant rather than close at hand!

There is another way to say this. If God is basically a Supreme Being who "merely exists," then we can give intellectual assent to God's existence. But we can also ignore such a God after having affirmed His existence. We can profess our faith in God's existence but then live as we want.

If God really is Yahweh, a God who really lives with us, then all this has to change. For we cannot walk away from a God who is always present to us. Wherever we go, there God goes. This God is not in a place; He is in relationship with people. Sooner or later we have to stop trying to escape from this God. We have to turn around and look within. We have to face the God who is always with us. Then we can live in that faith-trust-love covenant relationship that this God, Yahweh, so earnestly desires.

These are two of many reasons why God has so often repeated the consoling message implied in His name, Yahweh: I AM WITH YOU. He has expressed it in many different ways, hoping we will eventually believe Him to be Lord, a God-with-us. These are not empty arguments. For there is a bewildering fact. Even after centuries of Yahweh proclaiming His presence with us, Christians still do not really know God as Yahweh. Most Christians do not even know what His proper name is or even that He has one. Much less do they know what it means.

He has repeated His name to so many people and in so many situations. Yet Christians have little understanding of His name.

God could have referred to Himself as Yahweh only when speaking to Moses through the burning bush or only to Moses in his lifetime. In that case we would not need to give much attention to a God who called Himself Yahweh. But He has called Himself Yahweh frequently and consistently. It is time then to hear Him saying to us, "I am with you." It is time to realize that when He said to anyone in the past, "I am with you," He was already saying it to us today. With openness to God's continuing revelation of Himself today let us turn to some of His messages of former centuries.

### As I Was with Moses

Many texts show that God spoke to His people throughout the Old Testament just as He spoke to Moses. There are echoes and variations of the divine name, Yahweh, on every page of Scripture. In reading the Old Testament we note that they are but a commentary on God's revelation of Himself to us as Yahweh. They are the story of His efforts to bring us to faith in this mystery. Four Scripture passages representative of those which echo the Yahweh revelation are: Joshua 1:1–9; Jeremiah 1:4–8; Isaiah 41:8–14; and Isaiah 43:1–5.

The opening verses of the Book of Joshua show us what importance had already been given to the Yahweh revelation at this time:

> When Moses the servant of Yahweh was dead, Yahweh spoke to Joshua. . . . He said, "Moses my servant is dead; rise—it is time —and cross the Jordan here, you and all these people with you, into the land which I am giving the sons of Israel. Every place you tread with the soles of your feet I shall give you as I declared to Moses that I would. . . . As long as you live, no one shall be able to stand in your way: I will be with you as I was with Moses; I will not leave you or desert you." [1:1–3, 5.]

What impresses one immediately in this text is that God wastes no time, once Moses is dead, in continuing the work at hand. A sort of divine impatience is evident. "Rise, it is time," He says to Joshua. God is saying, "The work I wanted to do through Moses is done. Therefore, I have taken him to Myself. But there is other work that needs to be done; and you, Joshua, are the one through whom I wish to do it. And so, Joshua, let's get going. Rise up—it is time to get to work."

Why did God have to prod Joshua out of his hesitancy? Moses was truly a great man. He was the greatest of all the prophets. No other prophet reached the stature of his personality and the greatness of his mission. Yet God wastes no time in calling Joshua to rise from his grief and to begin immediately the unfinished work of Moses. God literally pushes Joshua onto the stage of salvation history to take over where Moses left off. God had taken away from the Israelites the greatest of their leaders, but He had someone waiting to replace him.

How differently we react when robbed of support and leadership, when a person of achievement is taken from our midst!

Often we succumb to grief, burdened by loss and overcome by self-pity. What does this kind of reaction really show? It shows that we have no deep faith in God as Lord. Our faith is instead in the human leader.

## No Time to Lose

An example from recent Church history has great similarity to the Moses-Joshua leadership replacement. The death of Pius XII was met with universal sorrow. A great pope, a true leader, had died. His passing was regarded as disastrous. Who could possibly replace him? Anxieties about the future of the Church were hardly allayed when Angelo Giuseppe Roncalli was elected pope and took the name John XXIII. Everyone called him an "interim" pope. Many were amused at his portly, nonpapal appearance. Now that John XXIII has passed on to God, however, we know he was indeed the man of the hour. God had him waiting to replace Pius XII just as He had Joshua waiting to replace Moses. God could use him because he had simple faith, deep humility, and a prayerful spirit.

His simple faith was tested one day as he was praying in the Benedictine Basilica of St. Paul outside the ancient walls of Rome. It was January 25, the feast of the Conversion of the great apostle Paul, and the last day of the Church Unity Octave. That day Pope John heard God say to him, "Convene a Council!" It took faith for John to believe that the Lord had spoken to him. But in simple faith he acted on what he heard.

The Council that resulted opened up the windows of the Church to let in the gentle but powerful winds of Yahweh's Spirit. That Council brought new life and new vision. Turmoil and frustration did accompany this changed life and vision, for the new cannot be born without some death to the old. It is hard to imagine what the Church would be like today if there had been no John XXIII and no Vatican II. God was being Lord of His Church, a God with His people. He was with Pius XII, but

He was also with John XXIII. He is always at work creating and fulfilling His plans to bring new life to His people.

Much happens when God is allowed to be Lord of His people. When we believe God to be Yahweh, we can face the future with confidence. Then no event is so tragic as to make us despair. We become more keenly aware of our limitations and weaknesses. We realize also that we cannot trust in ourselves or in human wisdom and strength. Faith in God as Yahweh gives courage and hope. With faith in Yahweh we find our darkest moments conquered by the brightness of His glory. The death of Moses was surely such a dark moment in human experience. For the people it was a dark hour indeed, but God used it to unfold a new phase of His work of love. "Moses, my servant, is dead. Rise, Joshua, it is time." God is Yahweh, Lord, always-with-His-people. At every moment of time He is at work doing something special and unique. He was at work in the death of Moses. He used his death to fulfill His vow to bring His people into the Promised Land. And so we heard God say to Joshua:

> "Be strong and stand firm, for you are the man to give this people possession of the land that I swore to their fathers I should give to them. Only be strong and stand firm and be careful to keep all the Law which my servant Moses laid on you. . . . Have I not told you: Be strong and stand firm? Be fearless then, be confident, for go where you will, Yahweh your God is with you." [Jos. 1:6–7, 9.]

No one had been closer to Moses than Joshua. He had been his assistant. Surely he saw the intimacy between Moses and Yahweh. Surely he witnessed Moses going again and again to the Tent of Meeting, there to encounter the living God dwelling with His people. Joshua saw what happened to Moses every time he spoke with God face to face as friend is wont to speak to friend. Surely Joshua must have felt very inferior to Moses. He felt incapable of following him in his office. But we of ourselves do not do God's work. Human talents are not the primary matter of concern. What matters is the will and plan of the God who is Lord. "You, Joshua, are the man."

There was to be no standing still in nostalgia or frustration because Moses had died. Yahweh had chosen a successor. His plan of action was clear and firm. Indecision, lack of determination, every weakness of character and purpose were out of place. Four times, in telling Joshua of his mission, Yahweh gives him affirmation: "Be strong," "stand firm," "be fearless," "be confident" (1:9). And He clearly gives the reason: "I will be with you as I was with Moses" (1:5b); "Go where you will, Yahweh your God is with you" (1:9b); "I will not . . . desert you" (1:5c).

God first revealed Himself as Yahweh to Moses. But the record of Scripture does not show that God ever spoke as clearly to Moses as He did to Joshua! God took great pains to make it clear to Joshua that he would not be inferior. God would be as much with him as He was with Moses. "I will be with you as I was with Moses." "I will not leave you or desert you." "Go where you will, Yahweh your God is with you." God takes every precaution to prevent us from assuming He was Lord only to Moses. He lets His people know that He not only was with Moses but intended to be a God with everyone.

Had God waited for centuries to say again, "I am with you," we could have some reason to doubt the importance of the message. But God left no room for doubt. He hastened to assure Joshua, "I really am Yahweh; I really am God always with you. Therefore, I was with Moses but I will be with you in the same way. You, too, will know and personally experience that I am Yahweh, that I am with you."

## Go Now . . .

God re-echoes this affirmation of being with us in chapter 1 of Jeremiah. We read there of God's call to Jeremiah to be His prophet:

> "Before I formed you in the womb I knew you;
> before you came to birth I consecrated you;
> I have appointed you as a prophet to the nations."
>
> [1:5.]

God issued His call to Jeremiah even before his birth. While Jeremiah was still a child, some time before he was a mature man, Yahweh informed him of this prebirth call. And Jeremiah cried out in response:

"Ah, Lord Yahweh; look, I do not know how to speak: I am a child!" [1:6.]

Jeremiah had no experience in speaking before groups of people. Yet the Lord was already calling him to be His prophet. Jeremiah was appalled at the very thought. He knew that as a prophet he would be required to speak frequently and without preparation to groups of all kinds, including those hostile to his message. Humanly speaking, Jeremiah was not the man God should have chosen. But salvation is God's work. Human inadequacy need not be an obstacle to God in the fulfillment of His work. Rather, it can be an aid when it disposes us to surrender ourselves in faith to the wisdom and power of God's Spirit. This is the faith to which Yahweh leads Jeremiah:

But Yahweh replied,
"Do not say, 'I am a child.'
Go now to those to whom I send you
and say whatever I command you.
Do not be afraid of them,
for I am with you to protect you—
it is Yahweh who speaks!"
[1:7–8.]

Yes, Yahweh is the God who is with His people. He is God now with Jeremiah. There is only one thing that this God has to say whenever He speaks to His people: "I am with you; therefore, do not be afraid! Do not fear and do not hesitate." This God-with-Jeremiah says to him, "You, Jeremiah, are not alone. It is not by your own wisdom and strength that you will be My prophet. Your lack of experience will not be a hindrance in the accomplishment of My work. Have faith in Me. I will be with you. I shall clearly give you the word I want you to speak in My name. You will never be in doubt about what I want you to say."

So did Yahweh speak to Joshua and Jeremiah. God continued to proclaim His Lordship with His people in Deutero-Isaiah— that is, chapters 40–55 of the Book of Isaiah. Repeatedly Yahweh assured His exiled people in Babylon that He had not deserted them. He was still with them. They thought He had deserted them, for were they not in exile in a foreign land, a land ruled by alien gods? Had they not left the land of Yahweh?

To understand their conviction that Yahweh had deserted them, we need to recall that the ancient peoples, all of them polytheists, believed that the gods of the nations had dominion only over designated portions of the earth. Yahweh was the God of the Hebrews. So they believed He had dominion only over the land He either had originally given them or had conquered for them in their wars. From the desolation of life in exile their prayerful cries of rejection pierced the heavens, as we read in Isaiah:

> . . . "Yahweh has abandoned me,
> the Lord has forgotten me."
> [49:14.]

## I Will Never Forget You

How often this was the cry of God's exiled people! But Yahweh answered every cry with a pledge of fidelity and caring love:

> Does a woman forget her baby at the breast,
> or fail to cherish the son of her womb?
> Yet even if these forget,
> I will never forget you.
> [Is. 49:15.]

And again:

> "Listen to me, House of Jacob,
> all you who remain of the House of Israel,
> you who have been carried since birth,
> whom I have carried since the time you were born.

In your old age I shall be still the same,
When your hair is gray I shall still support you.
I have already done so, I have carried you,
I shall still support and deliver you."

[Is. 46:3–4.]

If God is Yahweh, the only God, then how can He not be God
of His people even though they are now in exile? The time of the
Exile, therefore, became a great period for training in deeper
faith. What the plagues were for Moses personally, the Exile was
for the banished people. Through the bitter experience of the
Exile, which seemed to say God had rejected them, they came to
know God had not rejected them. They learned He truly was
their Lord.

You, Israel my servant,
Jacob whom I have chosen,
descendant of Abraham my friend.
You whom I brought from the confines of the earth
and called from the ends of the world;
you to whom I said, "You are my servant,
I have chosen you, not rejected you,"
*do not be afraid, for I am with you;*
*stop being anxious and watchful, for I am your God.*
I give you strength, I bring you help,
I uphold you with my victorious right hand. . . .
I tell you, "Do not be afraid,
I will help you."
Do not be afraid, Jacob, poor worm,
Israel, puny mite.
I will help you—it is Yahweh who speaks—
the Holy One of Israel is your redeemer.

[Is. 41:8–14, italics added.]

And another passage reads:

But now, thus says Yahweh,
who created you, Jacob,
who formed you, Israel:

Do not be afraid, for I have redeemed you;
I have called you by your name, you are mine.

Should you pass through the sea, I will be with you;
or through rivers, they will not swallow you up.
Should you walk through fire, you will not be scorched
and the flames will not burn you.
For I am Yahweh, your God,
the Holy One of Israel, your savior. . . .
You are precious in my eyes . . .
you are honored and I love you. . . .
Do not be afraid, for I am with you.

[Is. 43:1–5a.]

These two passages are among the most comforting and heart-moving in all of Scripture. They seem to come directly from the heart of the God who calls Himself Yahweh. What Scripture passages can equal these in poetic power, in loving imagery, in expressing the longing in the Divine Heart? How clearly they illustrate that God is with His people! He did not give His comforting message only to Moses. He gave it to everyone; He gave it to all of His people down through the centuries. He gave it to Joshua. He gave it to the judges. He gave it to the kings of Judah. He gave it especially to everyone of His prophets. He gave it to them not only as their personal message of comfort and strength but as the message which they, in His name, were to deliver to all of His people.

In the oracles of Deutero-Isaiah, the prophet who administered to the exiles in Babylon, Yahweh's message of hope finds its highest literary expression. I suggest you read and ponder frequently these oracles in chapters 40–55 of the Book of Isaiah. Here Yahweh repeatedly, either explicitly or in some variation, says to His people, "I am with you." What else could God, the Lord, really say to a people who were feeling rejected by Him? God is Lord; He is with His people. This is what He has to say over and over again. This is the fundamental message in the Old Testament. This is the only message that God, Yahweh, has for His people. It is the only message His people really need to hear, whatever the circumstances. I-AM-WITH-YOU. This is God's name. This is His message. The name is the message!

## There Is No Other

There is another point to emphasize. Deutero-Isaiah ministered to the Israelites in exile. That exile occasioned an agonizing
crisis of faith. Prior to it the Israelites lived a very superficial life.
They paid lip service to the Lord their God. They expected God
to be their Lord even when they did not live with Him or for
Him. This was the hypocritical faith and self-righteous way of
life that God called Jeremiah to expose. Many times Jeremiah invited the people to return, to fulfill their part of the covenant;
but return they would not. Yet they expected God as Yahweh to
defend their privileges and to uphold their cause. They were
guilty of presumption. Yahweh was God-with-them, was He not?
Did they not live in His land? Was not Jerusalem the city He
loved? How holy was His dwelling place in the Temple! How
could He let them be destroyed? How could He ever allow them
to be taken from His presence, to be driven from His land? Yet
here they were in a foreign land among an alien people. They
could only conclude that God had indeed abandoned them.

The Exile did occasion a crisis in faith. But it was also a price-
less experience. It led the people to a deeper faith, and to an expanded faith. They came to know not only that God was their
Lord and the Lord of their land. They came to know that He
was the only God. All the other gods were no gods at all! Until
this time the Israelites could and did accept the existence of
other gods. Yahweh had demanded of them by the first commandment not to go running after other gods but to worship
Him alone as their God. Now in exile they began to understand
what He was really saying. Yahweh, their God, was the only
God. So He was the God of all peoples and nations, including
their conquerors! Their anguish in feeling rejected turned into
the joy of a new acceptance. God, Yahweh, was still with them!
How heart-warming the divine assurances as they fell from the
lips of His prophets!

> Am I not Yahweh?
> There is no other god besides me,
> a God of integrity and a savior;
> There is none apart from me.
> Turn to me and be saved,
> All the ends of the earth,
> For I am God unrivaled.
>
> [Is. 45:21b–22.]

And again:

> I am God unrivaled,
> God who has no like.
> From the beginning I foretold the future. . . .
> I say: My purpose shall last.
>
> [Is 46:9–10.]

From this insight that Yahweh was the only God they came to a clear realization that He alone was the Creator God, the one who brought all things into being. Isaiah confirmed this for them:

> Who was it measured the water of the sea
>     in the hollow of his hand
> and calculated the dimensions of the heavens,
> gauged the whole earth to the bushel,
> weighed the mountains in scales,
>     the hills in a balance?
>
> Who could have advised the spirit of Yahweh,
> what counselor could have instructed him?
> Whom has he consulted to enlighten him,
> and to learn the path of justice
> and discover the most skillful ways?
> See, the nations are like a drop on the pail's rim,
> they count as a grain of dust on the scales. . . .
>
> To whom could you liken God?
> What image could you contrive of him? . . .
>
> Was it not told you from the beginning?
> Have you not understood how the earth was formed?
> He lives above the circle of the earth,

its inhabitants look like grasshoppers.
He has stretched out the heavens like a cloth,
spread them like a tent for men to live in. . . .

"To whom could you liken me
and who could be my equal?" says the Holy One.
[Is. 40:12–15a, 18, 21b–22, 25.]

From this insight the Israelites realized that their God was the only one at work in the history of the world, especially in their own history. They began to understand how wrong they were in thinking Yahweh had rejected them:

How can you insist, Israel,
"My destiny is hidden from Yahweh . . ."?
Did you not know?
Had you not heard?

Yahweh is an everlasting God,
he created the boundaries of the earth.
He does not grow tired or weary,
his understanding is beyond fathoming.
He gives strength to the wearied,
he strengthens the powerless.
Young men may grow tired and weary . . .
but those who hope in Yahweh renew their strength. . . .
They run and do not grow weary,
walk and never tire.

[Is. 40:27–31.]

## Variations on a Theme

These are comments on only four of many texts that could have been chosen to show how Yahweh has revealed Himself to His people. This precious message is expressed in ever so many ways. The Scriptures are a sort of symphony. Like the melody of a symphony they present a basic theme, the theme that God is Lord. As such He is with His people. But this theme has, as in a symphony, many variations. They give a richness, a power, and a beauty to the Scriptures. Unless the theme is known, one misses the variations and fails to sense the unity in the whole work. The unity of the Scriptures is ultimately the unity of the theme. All of Scripture is bound together into one book because it has but one message. That message is God's revelation of Himself as Lord: "I am who I am." "I am the God who is always with you, doing for you what needs to be done. I am with you to lead and guide, to empower and inspire. I am your God, personally, directly, and intimately."

So we can come to know what God is really like through believing what He has said about Himself. By this belief we find ourselves in intimate communion with God as our Lord. Because God is with us, such communion with Him becomes possible. The infinite gap between God and us, Creator and creature, is bridged because of who God is. God is Himself the bridge over the gap precisely because He is God-with-us. When we by faith accept God as God-with-us, the bridge over the gap has been built. The mystery is that God and we become one in a communion of life. For God is God-with-us.

This mystery not only establishes the possibility of a union between God and us. It also determines the qualities and characteristics of such a life. Many such characteristics could be noted, but there is one which is highlighted in each of the four chosen texts. If God is truly always with us, then we, having God always with us, should have a life free of fear and full of courage.

"I am with you; do not be afraid." Almost every time God assures us of His presence, He adds immediately, "Do not be afraid." Life with God is characterized primarily by an absence of fear. There is no surer proof that Jews and Christians do not believe in the Lordship of their God than the existing fear in their hearts, minds, and souls.

God made us to His own image and likeness. We were not meant to be lonely. We are to live in loving, trusting relationship with others. We are to live under the wise and loving Lordship of our God and Creator. By so doing we will have no fear. For God is with us and Yahweh, our Lord, has our life totally in His almighty hands.

Fear arises from feeling alone and feeling responsible for situations over which we have little or no control. We are so weak and ignorant. We are so helpless. Yet we burden ourselves with the responsibility of trying to control our lives and all situations. Since there is no way of obtaining such control, we are afraid.

But God says to us, "Do not be afraid. For I am Lord. As Lord, I am in total control of everything. I do not take away anyone's freedom. But I am wise and strong enough to use every incident, whether directly willed by Me or merely permitted by Me; I can use everything for the good of those who will let Me be their Lord. So believe that I am your Lord, that I am with you; and then you will be rid of all your fears of whatever kind. For I will take care of you."

Do we begin to see how important the Lordship of God is? It is the only basis for the elimination of the greatest enemy of man: fear! God Himself knows this. So He says over and over, "I am with you. Do not be afraid."

Freedom from fear is one side of the coin of true faith in the Lordship of God. The other side of the coin is courage. If God is with us now and we face the future with Him, we can have the courage to move forward in hope. Persons of faith in God as Lord entrust everything to this God who is with them and for them. Such people have God's wisdom and strength. They do not hold themselves responsible for the tasks in life; rather, God is responsible. They seek only to be open channels and fit instruments. They move forward with God's power and wisdom. Nothing daunts them, nothing discourages them. They are not alone. They have Someone with them, Someone reliable and dependable, Someone almighty and all wise, Someone all merciful and all loving. This Someone is the God who claims to be their Lord, Yahweh, God-with-them.

What this God said to Joshua He says to everyone: "Have I not told you: Be strong and stand firm? Be fearless then, be confident, for go where you will, Yahweh your God is with you" (Jos. 1:9).

This then is the message I give you in the name of God who is our Lord and Father: "I am with you; do not be afraid; be strong and stand firm. As long as you live, no one shall be able to stand in your way; I will be with you as I was with Moses; I will not leave you or desert you. For I am Yahweh, the Lord your God."

# CHAPTER III

# A Man Like Us

The mystery that our God is a God-with-us is expressed in His proper name, Yahweh, Lord. This name, because it is God's proper name, accurately reveals the divine nature. It gives us the essential dimension of the divine life. Yahweh, our God, has not chosen to live in distant aloofness from us. He is with us and for us. However, while being with us and for us, He remains God. Even though He has been God-with-us through the ages since Moses, He has not lost any of His divine prerogatives. He is as much God now as He was before He revealed Himself as being in our midst. We can say, therefore, that there are two essential elements in the mystery of God as Yahweh. First, He is truly God, totally divine. Secondly, He is truly with us, totally taken up with our cause. He is "on our side," as St. Paul affirms. He is not against us.

So much has already been said about God, Yahweh, our Lord! So much more could be said about this God-with-us! We have stated that the Lordship of God is the basic revelation in the Old Testament. This mystery is the foundation faith for Christianity. Christians must come to know God as Lord. Without belief in God as Lord we cannot understand the deepest significance of Christianity.

God, in revealing Himself as Yahweh, makes demands on peo-

ple who believe He is with them. For example, the person of
faith responds by laying aside all fears and courageously facing
the challenges of life. Many other points could be made showing
how God's revelation of Himself as Yahweh affects every aspect
of life. But it is now important for us to build on the foundation
of the Yahweh revelation. We need to understand that the central message of the New Testament is also one of Lordship, the
Lordship of Jesus.

In focusing on Jesus, we do not abandon the theme of God as
Yahweh. For God came to be with us in an absolutely unique
way through Christ. Indeed, *Jesus, the Christ, is the fullest revelation to us of the God who proclaims Himself to be Yahweh,
Lord.* More importantly, Jesus, the man born of Mary and the
son of the Eternal Father, became Lord through His rising from
the dead. God, in other words, is now Yahweh for us *inasmuch*
as Jesus, the man, is Yahweh, God-with-us. For Jesus, risen from
the dead, has entered into full possession, through the Spirit, of
all the powers and privileges of God as Yahweh.

The descendants of Moses, those to whom the Yahweh message was first revealed, are the Jews of today. Seemingly, of all
peoples, the Jews should have the strongest faith in Jesus as Yahweh. But this very faith in Jesus as Lord has caused division between Christians and Jews. We believe Jesus to be the Christ,
the one spoken of by the prophets of old. With the exception of
that one small remnant, the messianic Jews, all others deny that
Jesus is Lord. Yet this belief could be our strongest source of
unity, if Christians truly believed with the Jews that the God
who is, is Yahweh.

We can no longer speak of the God of Abraham, Isaac, and
Jacob merely as "God." God identified Himself as the one who
had appeared to Abraham, Isaac, and Jacob. But He also has
revealed Himself as I AM WHO I AM, or Yahweh. Yahweh is the
God of the Jews. Yahweh is the God of all Christians. If we
Christians really knew God as Lord, Yahweh, the Jews could feel
a deep kinship with us. We could come to Jesus with them in
unity since, in the name of Yahweh, Jesus would be our Lord
and theirs. There is a vast difference between knowing God as

some kind of supreme being and knowing Him as God-with-us. If we knew Him as God-with-us, we would likewise approach Jesus from this perspective of faith. We could then accept Jesus as He was given to us by the Lord God, His Father.

## A Perfect Man?

Our God is not just God. He is God-with-us. A similar statement can be made about Jesus. Our faith is not merely that Jesus is a perfect man. Our faith, rather, is that Jesus is a man like us in all things but sin. The statement "Jesus is perfect man," is meant to uphold the humanity of Jesus. But it can also make a denial of His humanity very easy. It could be understood this way: Jesus has a complete human nature. He has all the essential components of a human being—a body and a soul, and all the powers belonging to each. He has these organs in a "perfect" state. Jesus would accordingly be the "perfect" man.

The Scriptures do not speak of Jesus as being "perfect" in this manner. The Scriptures stress not so much that He is "perfect" as that He is "true," real, authentic. The mark of His authenticity is His identity with us. We know from daily experience what we are like. If Jesus were too much unlike us, we would have to question whether He is really a man, a human being. But He is like us. This is what the Scriptures stress.

We Christians, however, have not been stressing this dimension of the humanity of Jesus. We have stressed His divinity. Anyone who speaks about His humanity with the frankness of the New Testament is met with suspicion. Many fear that such a person is denying the divinity of Jesus.

The assumption is that by making Jesus more human we make Him less divine. So we safely uphold His divinity by pronouncing in neat, abstract terms that He is a "perfect man" This term, "perfect man," can be given a correct, orthodox interpretation. But it also provides an escape from the necessity of being confronted with the stark reality of the "humanness of the humanity" of Jesus.

God in His Holy Word does not allow us this easy escape. The
New Testament speaks bluntly of the humanity of Jesus. As
Christians we are abysmally unaware of this New Testament
message. Many were shocked by the language of the rock opera
*Jesus Christ Superstar*. Whatever might be the faith of its authors, this opera sings authentically of Jesus, the man. Its very
language is borrowed from the New Testament.

Christians need to know what the New Testament says about
the humanity of Jesus. There is no need to hide either the true
humanity or the divinity of Jesus if we know these Scriptures.
Most of the New Testament writers knew Jesus well. They knew
Him from the experience of personal contact, or they were at
most only one generation removed from Him. They knew what
He was like experientially. They knew how He lived, what He
endured. They report what they saw with a refreshing honesty.
They record a contemporary vision of Jesus. Unless we base our
faith on their record, we believe in a Jesus of our imagination.
Four texts from their writings speak of Jesus as a man-like-us
and do so with clarity and completeness: one from Philippians
and three from Hebrews.

In the first text, from Philippians, Paul is very probably quoting from an early Christian hymn. This testimony of faith dates
from the Church shortly after Pentecost. Paul quotes this hymn
with complete approval. He writes of Jesus:

> His state was divine,
> yet he did not cling
> to his equality with God
> but emptied himself
> to assume the condition of a slave,
> and became as men are;
> and being as all men are,
> he was humbler yet,
> even to accepting death,
> death on a cross.
>
> [2:6–8.]

This passage is an explicit profession of faith in the divinity of
Jesus Christ. "His state was divine." But this statement also

boldly acclaims His humanity. It clearly asserts that Jesus "did not cling to His equality with God, but emptied Himself." While He was here on earth, Jesus never demanded the rights He had as God. Whatever rights He had as God were given up. He surrendered them precisely so that He could assume the condition of slave and become like us in all things.

## He Emptied Himself

What was this equality with God of which He "emptied Himself"? The "emptying" spoken of here could not refer to His divine nature and personality. God cannot give away any attribute of His divinity. God is God and will always remain who He is. The "emptying," therefore, had to be something that took place in the humanity of Jesus. What could this something be?

Jesus had the right, because He was the Son of God, to come into the world in such a way as to be able to manifest His divinity to all. This manifestation of divinity would have been through some unique quality present in His human nature. From the New Testament we learn that this unique quality of human nature is the state of glorification. It is that state which Jesus miraculously enjoyed for a few brief moments during the Transfiguration on Mount Tabor. It is that state which Jesus now enjoys eternally, in having risen from the dead to the glory of God, His Father and Lord.

To this state of glory, that of bodily glorification, Jesus had a right. He was the Incarnate Son of God. Being the Son of God, He had the right to let His divine life shine through His body without any diminishment. He would have thus been a true, perfect man. But He would have been very much unlike the rest of us! In coming into the world to save us, He laid aside this glory. He came into the world without it. He did not cling to His equality with God. Rather, He decided to cling to His equality with us. He became one of us, like us in all things. He truly was now God-with-us!

Being God-with-us, Jesus gave up what He is now, what He

has now as Risen Lord. What He gave up was rightfully His from the very moment of His conception by Mary under the power of the Holy Spirit. At the moment of becoming a man, Jesus emptied Himself of this state of glory. He did not take it on. To do so would have prevented Him from having a human nature capable of sharing in our human condition. Saint Paul says, quoting this early Christian hymn, that He "emptied himself to assume the condition of a slave, and [thus He] became as men are."

This text is already asserting what the three texts chosen from Hebrews will assert more explicitly: There is an identity of the human condition of Jesus with all of us. Jesus did not merely assume our nature. He assumed it in such a way that He, as a man, shared the same human condition as all of us. He was not less a man but more a man. He was not less human but more human. He was not less involved in the human situation but more involved. There is no human being who has more completely subsumed into his personal realm of human experience our sinful lot than did the man, Jesus.

## The Slave of Mankind

This is why we must assert that Jesus became not merely a man but the slave of mankind. He became the lowest and the least of men. He "emptied himself to assume the condition of a *slave*, and became *as men are;* and being as all men are, he was humbler yet, even to accepting death, death on a cross." What this text is trying to highlight is the lowly and humble condition of the human nature assumed by Jesus. He came in such a condition that He knew He had to be the slave of others. He had to be more lowly and humble than others. He knew He had no wish to escape from the task of giving His life for others. The condition of His human nature committed Him to death—not just any kind of death but death in the most ignominious manner then known, death on a cross. Any other form of death would have been less generous for Him.

St. Paul emphasizes often the degree to which Jesus became
one of us:

> For our sake God made the sinless one into sin, so that in him we
> might become the goodness of God. [2 Co. 5:21.]

This is a strong statement. The question is, how was Jesus
"made into sin"? For if there is one thing certain about Jesus, it
is that He was sinless; He never committed any personal sin. Yet
Paul clearly affirms He was made "into sin" for our sake. How?
We have the explanation in our interpretation of the passage
from Philippians: In *not* coming into our midst in a human nature graced with the glory of God; in *coming* into our midst in a
human nature emptied of that glory of God, Jesus came into a
condition that enabled Him to experience the human *sinful* condition. He was personally sinless. The *guilt* of personal sin never
once in the slightest degree clouded His soul.

Yet He as man, totally free from sin in the sight of God, was
totally unfree from the ravages and consequences of sin upon
human nature. There is no human state between sin and glory. If
Jesus had come in glory, He would not have experienced our sinful condition in His body, soul, or even in His spirit. It is His
unglorified state which is then the way in which He was made
into sin for us. Being without that glory, He was liable to sin's
ravages, the principal one of which is *death*. Now that Jesus is in
glory, He cannot die. This is the clear teaching of Paul in
Romans 6:9-10:

> Christ, as we know, having been raised from the dead will never
> die again. Death has no power over him any more. When he
> died, he died, once for all, to sin, so his life now is life with God.

Paul here states that, in dying, Jesus died to sin. Paul is in
effect saying that, in dying, Jesus died to death. He died in such
a way that He would never again experience death. For when
Jesus rose from the dead, He did not merely come back to *this*
life, the life He had lived. With such a life He would have had to
die again, since this life is one of sin. But He died to sin. So He
rose to a totally new life, a life freed from sin and death. Jesus

risen from the dead is immortal; He cannot die. Death is no longer a human possibility for Jesus. The *glorified* condition in which His bodily frame now exists makes death an impossibility.

It was this glorified state which Jesus laid aside. He emptied Himself of it. He never clung to it once while here on earth. He did not claim it as His right. He saw Himself, though sinless, as one with all sinners. He bore the consequences of their sin in His body. In their name He humbled Himself before His God and theirs. He took responsibility for the sin of all mankind, and experienced their sin personally in His own mortal, vulnerable condition. He felt and knew He was *no better* than anyone else: "Being as all men are, he was humbler yet" (Ph. 2:7-8). In this humility, in this honesty of truth, He felt bound to give His life in expiation for sin, for all sin. He gave His life not just through any kind of death but through a death that would manifest the hideousness of all sin: ". . . he was humbler yet, even to accepting death, death on a cross."

In the Prologue to his Gospel, St. John emphasizes the degree to which Jesus became human:

> In the beginning was the Word:
> the Word was with God
> and the Word was God. . . .
> The Word was made flesh.
> [1:1, 14.]

St. John does not hesitate to use the graphic word "flesh" to express his understanding of the mystery of the Incarnation. As he uses "flesh" here instead of "man," so likewise he uses "flesh" instead of "body" in reference to the Eucharist (6:51). "Flesh" in the Scriptures is an important theological word designating the whole of the individual, or at times, of humankind in general. It is a state of deprivation of the glory of God through the loss of His Spirit.

Jesus is flesh in that He emptied Himself of that full glorification by the Spirit to which He was entitled. Inasmuch as His body was not glorified by the Spirit, His body was subject to some of the consequences of sin. This is what enabled Him to have a human nature which was so much like that of other human beings. The idea is stressed by the author of the letter to the Hebrews. We wish to comment on three texts from this letter which refer to the humanity of Jesus.

These three texts describe forcefully and progressively some of the implications of the mystery of the human condition of the body of Jesus. Through the first text the identity of the human condition between Jesus and the rest of humankind is established. The purposes for this identity are also stated:

> As it was his [the Father's] purpose to bring a great many of his sons into glory, it was appropriate that God . . . should make perfect, through suffering, the leader who would take them to their salvation. For the one who sanctifies, and the ones who are sanctified, are of the same stock; that is why he openly calls them *brothers.* . . . Since all the *children* share the same blood and flesh, he too shared equally in it, so that by his death he could take away all the power of the devil, who had power over death, and set free all those who had been held in slavery all their lives by the fear of death. For it was not the angels that he took to himself; he took to himself *descent from Abraham.* It was essential that he should in this way become completely like his brothers so that he could be a compassionate and trustworthy high priest of God's religion, able to atone for human sins. That is, because he has himself been through temptation he is able to help others who are tempted. [Heb. 2:10–11, 14–18.]

Though this passage is self-explanatory it deserves additional comment. Any form of denial of the depths to which the Son of God took on human flesh is a distortion of the Father's plan for saving man. Any form of denial is also a failure to accept Jesus as the Father gave Him to us. Such denial prevents us from really knowing both Jesus, as God's Son, and the Father as God Himself. Christians have suffered much from the lack of an appropriate faith in Jesus. True faith in Jesus must accept the depths to which He identified Himself with all human beings in the "sinful" condition in which He assumed His human nature. The author of Hebrews had this faith in the humanity of Jesus. He states this faith in four remarkable ways in this passage.

## The Same Flesh and Blood

First, Jesus is truly our brother. He has the *same* blood and the *same* flesh that we do. He is, moreover, proud of the fact He is our brother. He looks upon us as His brothers and sisters. He loves to call us His brothers and sisters. He boasts of the fact He is of the same stock that we are. He is our brother and we are His brothers and sisters because we all share the same condition of flesh and blood.

## A Member of Our Race

Secondly, Jesus is a member of the human race. He is a descendant of Abraham. It would have been possible for God to have His Son become man by creating for Him a human body in a way other than from woman. Jesus in that case would have been a perfect man. He would have had a complete human nature. But He would not have been our Savior and Redeemer. For His salvific work He had to assume *our* human flesh and blood. He had to be born as all men are born, of woman. He thus had to become a member of the human race. Jesus, in being born of woman, has a human genealogy. He has a human mother who conceived Him, bore Him, gave Him birth, nursed Him, taught Him. He has a human though virginal father. He has grandparents on both sides. He is, therefore, a descendant of David, of Abraham, and of Adam.

Are we belaboring the obvious? No, because we are always beset by the tendency to ignore the fleshly condition of Jesus as man. We tend to hyperspiritualize the humanity of Jesus, to "angelize" Him. But "it was not the angels that he took to himself." Jesus did not become an angel. He did not live an angelic life. He became a man, a human being. He lived a human life, our life, the life of our race. He truly shared our flesh and our blood, and did so *equally*. No exception was made in this regard, except one: personal sin. It was by taking descent from Abraham that He became completely like us, His brothers and sisters.

Thirdly, was this complete identity with the human condition necessary? Could not Jesus have dispensed with it? No! "It was essential that he should in this way become completely like his brothers." If Jesus had not become completely like us, He could not have been our Savior. But, to accept Him now as our Savior, we must in turn accept His humanness. Too many Christians pay mere lip service to the humanity of Christ and know Jesus only as divine. That is not the real Jesus. Faith in that kind of Jesus does not beget an authentic Christian faith or a vibrant Christian life.

Why was this complete identity of Jesus with the human condition so essential? "So that he could be a compassionate and trustworthy high priest of God's religion, able to atone for human sins."

## A Compassionate Savior

Jesus, to be our Savior and High Priest, had to have a body of flesh and a soul of human spirit. He needed them in such a way that He could feel what we feel, suffer what we suffer, experience what we experience. He needed them in such a way that He could *feel* our suffering. He needed them in such a way that He could be *moved to pity* over our pain and anguish. It is not enough for Jesus to know that we are suffering. He needs to do more than give us counsel from the distance of a stoic uninvolvement.

Only if He is completely like us can He be trustworthy, worthy of our faith and trust. How hard it would be to put faith and trust in Jesus *as our Savior* if He were completely removed from our human condition! Trustworthiness implies identity of experience. We can have faith in Him and surrender to Him in trust only because we know He has been one with us in every tribulation and joy.

The author shows his faith in the humanity of Jesus in a fourth way. "That is, because he has himself been through temptation he is able to help others who are tempted." We were redeemed because Jesus was one with us in our human condition. That He was the Son of God is extremely important. But our redemption was accomplished by the *Incarnate* Son of God. Because the Son of God in His human flesh endured and overcame the same temptations we have, He is able to help us when we endure those temptations.

For years I was told, "When tempted call on Jesus, for He is God. He as God can help you." But *my* greatest source of help comes from knowing that Jesus, being the God-man, has endured and overcome the same temptations that I have. I can be victorious over them with His strength. I let myself be more open to His victorious power if I call upon Him in His victory over temptations. That is what makes Him worthy of our trust.

## A Trustworthy High Priest

The second of our three chosen texts from Hebrews continues this thought of trust in the humanity of Jesus.

> We must never let go of the faith that we have professed. For it is not as if we had a high priest who was incapable of feeling our weaknesses with us; but we have one who has been tempted in every way that we are, though he is without sin. Let us be confident, then, in approaching the throne of grace, that we shall have mercy from him and find grace when we are in need of help. [4:14–16.]

Note that the faith we are urged never to let go of is faith in the ability of Jesus to feel our weakness with us. This is what gives the Christian, the believer in Jesus, such deep consolation. He knows he has a high priest who understands, and does so not merely in a perfectly intellectual manner but also on the gut level of human emotions, on the gut level of knowing what we are going through because He can recall His own identical experiences.

At this point our tendency is to respond, "Yes, but. . . . He can feel some of our weaknesses with us, but not all of them." Hence our author continues, "But we have [a high priest] who has been tempted in every way that we are, though he is without sin." If we are able to be helped in our temptations because He has Himself been through temptation, then the fact that He has been tempted in every way we are becomes extremely important. It becomes our source of victory in every possible temptation. More importantly, it undergirds and supports a life of total faith and trust in Jesus. I don't need a Savior who blesses me only if I first prove myself worthy, only if I first become "good" by my own strength. What I need is a Savior who deigns to accept me as weak and sinful, one who can understand me in my weakness and sinfulness, one who will give me His strength when I am weak. This is Jesus: and in such a Savior I can trust. In such a Savior I *will* trust.

> Let us be confident, then, in approaching the throne of grace, that we shall have mercy from him and find grace when we are in need of help.

Our third chosen text from Hebrews speaks of His prayer.

> During his life on earth, he offered up prayer and entreaty, aloud and in silent tears, to the one who had the power to save him out of death, and he submitted so humbly that his prayer was heard. Although he was Son, he learned to obey through suffering; but having been made perfect, he became for all who obey him the source of eternal salvation and was acclaimed by God with the title of high priest *of the order of Melchizedek*. [5:7–10.]

In this passage the depths to which Jesus in His human nature assumed the weaknesses and agonies of our "sinful" human condition is evident: Jesus prayed! The Gospels are too clear on this point for us to be able to deny it. But why did Jesus pray? Do we explain His prayer in terms of "setting us a good example," implying there was no real need for Him to pray for Himself? Did He just put on a nice demonstration of prayer for us? Did He go through the motions of praying and then say to us, "Here

is how you go about it"? This kind of attitude is an effective denial of the depths to which Jesus assumed our human condition.
This is drawing wrong conclusions from the mystery of His divinity.

## He Had to Pray

Jesus prayed because He *had* to. Jesus prayed because He
was, like us, constantly dependent on His heavenly Father for
love and solace, for wisdom and strength, for grace and power.
He was always in need of His Father to be with Him. At the critical moments of His life, when decisions had to be made affect-
ing the course of His ministry, He was even more dependent on
heavenly guidance. And at those times He was more in need of
prayer than ever.

The prayer of Jesus to His Father reflected His life experiences. It was not always the prayer of ecstatic union. Often it
was the prayer of crushing agony and dark despair. As He
prayed He gave expression to every human emotion. No man
was more emotional than Jesus. No man's prayer has ever been
as filled with true emotion as the prayer of Jesus. At times the
pain or the joy was so intense that He had to cry aloud. At other
times the pain or the joy was so deep that all He could do was
shed silent tears. We will know Jesus to be a man like us in all
things but sin when we perceive, in faith, the mystery of His
prayer.

There is one other thought not explicitly mentioned but almost
demanded by each of these four texts. Because Jesus was the
man that He was, He had to walk by trust in Yahweh and by
faith in His word. If He did not have to live by faith and trust,
He was not a man like us.

Our life as human beings is one of faith in each other. Our life
as Christians is one of trust in Jesus and of faith in His word. By
trusting His fidelity to His word we are led to surrender to His
will.

The life of Jesus was no different. He, too, walked by faith, by trust. He sought out the word of Yahweh, His Father. He searched for that word every morning as He got up, every hour as He went about His work. When He heard the Father speak to Him, He accepted the word heard in faith and carried it out. While He was here on earth, He did not walk in the vision of glory; He walked in the light of the vision of faith. So we can truly affirm with the author of Hebrews that He was a man like us in all things but sin. This is why at each Eucharist we can strongly profess our belief that Jesus, too, walked by faith:

> He was conceived through the power of the Holy Spirit, and born of the Virgin Mary, a man like us in all things but sin.

## Immanuel

We must conclude that the Incarnate Son of God reveals God to us. Our God is God-with-us. He is Yahweh, Lord. The Incarnate Son assumed a human nature just like ours because it was the clearest way of manifesting a God whose inner life longs for fellowship with us. Once we even faintly grasp the mystery of the Lordship of God, we begin to see that God could not have been satisfied by having His Son become a man perfect and whole. He had to be a man like us in all things except sin. Only such a man could witness to the nature of God as a God-with-man. Any other kind of Savior would not have proved the meaning of His proper name, Yahweh. How could we have believed God to be Lord, with His people, if He had assumed a human nature not limited by our human condition? He, though a perfect man, would not really have been one of us. He would have been an Incarnate Son looking on from the outside, unable to identify with us in our condition, unable to experience what we feel. He would have continued to cling to His equality with God as He lived in our midst. He would have been among us but not a part of us, for there would not have been that self-emptying which allowed Him to assume the condition of a slave. He would have been a perfect man, a true man, but not a pilgrim member of our race. He would not have shared our mortal flesh and blood. He would not have been as all other men are. He would not have been as lowly as we are.

Christians are more than theists. Most human beings believe in the existence of a God. But as Christians we believe much more. We believe the one and only true God is a God-with-us. We know this only because He revealed it about Himself. Because of this revelation our faith is inadequate unless we really accept the mystery of His Lordship and surrender to all of its implications. This acceptance and surrender is the Christian life.

One manifestation of the Lordship of God is fundamental to all the others. It is the Incarnation, the mystery of God's Son becoming a son of man. Jesus is this Incarnate Son. Everything about Him, not merely His doctrine but the way He lived, the very condition of His human flesh, manifests the mystery of the Godhead. We really know God is with us when we look at Jesus, the God-man, and see that He is a person like us in all things but sin. Then we know that God is Yahweh, for Jesus truly is Immanuel. This is our faith. This is our joy. This is ultimately why we are a people of praise, a people always singing a new song to the Lord!

There are many joys in the Christian life. It is so easy to assume that such joys are manifestations of God, His love and presence, but that sorrows and hardships are not. However, the way Jesus assumed His human nature should negate such an idea. If God is with us, He will most certainly be with us in time of trial and tribulation, of misfortune and misunderstanding. And if He is *then* with us, we have through our faith assurance that God is Lord, the source of an inconquerable courage, long-suffering and hope. We have a faith that gives rise to a victorious life, to healing through His power. Then we can say with St. Paul from the very core of our being:

> With God on our side who can be against us? Since God did not spare his own Son, but gave him up to benefit us all, we may be certain, after such a gift, that he will not refuse anything he can give. . . .
>
> Nothing therefore can come between us and the love of Christ,

even if we are troubled or worried, or being persecuted, or lacking food or clothes, or being threatened or even attacked. As scripture promised: *For your sake we are being massacred daily and reckoned as sheep for the slaughter.* These are the trials through which we triumph, by the power of him who loved us.

For I am certain of this: neither death nor life, no angel, no prince, nothing that exists, nothing still to come, not any power, or height or depth, nor any created thing, can come between us and the love of God made visible in Christ Jesus our Lord. [Rom. 8:31–32, 35–39.]

The human nature of Jesus manifests to us that He is equally and completely like us, His brothers and sisters. He has shared our flesh and blood; therefore, He can be our compassionate and trustworthy high priest able to atone for our sins!

# CHAPTER IV

# "You Are the Christ"

When I was younger I often wondered what the title *Christ* meant. *Jesus* I could understand. It means "Savior," and "Savior" was one who could help me when I was in trouble. But the word *Christ:* Could it be the family name of Jesus as Tunink was mine? Later I came to know that *Christ* is the Greek translation of the Hebrew word *Messiah*, "the Anointed One." But even then the full title *Jesus Christ* meant no more to me than just the name *Jesus.* That is, until a few years ago.

I have come to realize that Christians need to know more about Jesus than that He is true God and true man. He is a man like us in all things but sin; He emptied Himself of divine glory in order to become a slave. But I now realize that to understand the Christian life we need to know what is meant by Jesus as the Christ. This is because a Christian is a follower of Jesus *as the Christ.* So I searched for an understanding of the title *Christ.* I learned that to speak of Jesus as the Christ means to speak of the role of the Holy Spirit in His life. It means to accept the life of Jesus as being "in the Spirit." As the Christ, Jesus is the One who was always anointed by the Spirit of God.

## The Basic Manifestation

The Gospels describe many manifestations of the Spirit in the life of Jesus. But the basic manifestation of the Spirit in Him is His weakness and His identity with us in our human condition. This Spirit of Yahweh overshadowed Mary and she conceived Jesus, the Incarnate Son. The Spirit was responsible for the condition of the human nature that Jesus received through her. Jesus was driven by the Spirit into the desert to be *tempted by Satan!* The author of Hebrews tells us, "Christ . . . offered himself as the perfect sacrifice to God through the eternal Spirit" (9:14). The temptations of Jesus and His sacrificial death on the Cross are attributed to this messianic Spirit moving in Him. Is it not that same Spirit at work in all the other manifestations of the humanness of Jesus? In His fatigue at Jacob's well? In His tears? In His joy and humor? In His love for little children? In His friendships? In the difficulties He had in obeying His Father's will? In the abandonment He endured on the Cross? In His ability to feel our weakness with us?

It was truly the Holy Spirit who moved the man Jesus, born of Mary to be a man like us in all things but sin. But that same Holy Spirit in many ways is at work in our lives. The Spirit conforms us to Christ in His weakness, in His sufferings, and in His death. The reality of weakness, suffering, and death is hard to accept in our lives of union with Jesus. But we can be Christians now precisely because we too can be anointed by the same Spirit who anointed Jesus in His weakness. The action of the Holy Spirit can be on us too in our periods of weakness just as on Jesus in His weakness, temptations, and sufferings.

The Spirit is a source of divine power *in human weakness*. The prophet Isaiah announces that the messianic King to come will be anointed by the Spirit of Yahweh. His prophetic words describe the inner strength of moral righteousness of this Messiah. He tells us that the Spirit with all of His gifts will rest on

that Messiah, the descendant of Jesse, who is one day to sit on
the throne of David:

> A shoot springs from the stock of Jesse,
> a scion thrusts from his roots:
> on him the spirit of Yahweh rests,
> a spirit of wisdom and insight,
> a spirit of counsel and power,
> a spirit of knowledge and of the fear of Yahweh.
>
> [11:1–2.]

## Power Within Weakness

Isaiah then describes the kind of life this Spirit-filled Messiah
will live, what inner strength will be His:

> He does not judge by appearances,
> he gives no verdict on hearsay,
> but judges the wretched with integrity,
> and with equity gives a verdict for the poor of the land.
> His word is a rod that strikes the ruthless,
> his sentences bring death to the wicked.
> Integrity is the loincloth round his waist,
> faithfulness the belt about his hips.
>
> [11:3–5.]

This prophecy of Isaiah gives a perfect picture of Jesus. Each
of the Gospels authenticates this picture of Jesus. Indeed, Jesus
is the Christ, the man anointed by the fullness of the Spirit of
Yahweh!

Deutero-Isaiah, in the first of the four Suffering Servant songs,
also describes the Christ. This passage simply announces that
this servant of Yahweh will be given the Spirit:

> Here is my servant whom I uphold,
> my chosen one in whom my soul delights.
> I have endowed him with my spirit,
> that he may bring true justice to the nations.
>
> [Is. 42:1.]

Yahweh refers to these words of His prophet at the baptism of Jesus, and again at His Transfiguration, when he says about Jesus: "This is my Son, the Beloved. Listen to him" (Mk. 9:8). The Gospels confirm that Jesus is the Chosen one, the One to whom the Spirit is given, not for His own personal enjoyment but unto mission. That Spirit enabled Him to be the Savior of the world "that he may bring true justice to the nations."

A person so described would raise in us great expectations. Deutero-Isaiah seems to sense our expectations as noted in the Suffering Servant song:

> He does not cry out or shout aloud,
> or make his voice heard in the streets.
> He does not break the crushed reed,
> nor quench the wavering flame.
> Faithfully he brings true justice;
> he will neither waver, nor be crushed
> until true justice is established on earth.
>
> [42:2-4.]

The Spirit responsible for the Son of God taking on a human nature not "incapable of feeling our weakness with us" (Heb. 4:15) did support this man with inner strength. The Spirit filled Him with a meekness, a self-control, and a respect and delicateness for the weakness of others. For it was the task of Jesus to save and to heal, to encourage, and to bring back to life. He had to be strong enough not to be crushed Himself, but weak enough to understand the weakness of men. The Spirit is manifested in Jesus not only in all the actions which obviously are acts of power and might. He is manifested also in all those areas in which Jesus is truly one of us.

## The Child Grew

With this as a background we can better understand St. Luke's descriptions of the life of Jesus prior to His public ministry. He summarizes the first twelve years as follows:

> Meanwhile the child grew to maturity, and he was filled with
> wisdom; and God's favor was with him. [2:40.]

And the next eighteen years are described thus:

> And Jesus increased in wisdom, in stature, and in favor with God
> and men. [2:52.]

According to Luke, the principal characteristic of the life of
Jesus before the time of His public ministry was growth. This
growth was evident in all the dimensions of His human existence. He grew in body and age. This was so evident that Luke
does not even mention it. He grew to maturity. He passed
through all the stages of psychological development: infancy,
childhood, adolescence, and manhood.

But Jesus also grew in two other areas of His human existence: in holiness and in knowledge. This growth is more easily
understood if one sees it as the effect and ever-deepening action
of the Spirit upon His humanity. Never for one moment was
Jesus not as holy as He should have been. But He did *grow* in
holiness. As Jesus grew, He developed in His relationship with
His Father. This relationship is the work of the Spirit, for the
Spirit is relationship. He who is the bond between the Father
and the Son is the one who revealed to the Incarnate Son, Jesus,
*as He grew up*, the relationship that He had with Yahweh His
Father.

We see that Jesus at the age of twelve had an experience of
Yahweh as His Father far beyond the experience of other boys
His age. Yet, according to Luke, Jesus was in an early stage of
development in this relationship. Was this not partly the reason
for the ensuing eighteen years of the so-called hidden life? During these years Jesus awakened to a realization of who He was.
He struggled with this awareness to incorporate it into His self-
identity and into His style of life. The relationship which He as
Incarnate Son of God had with His Father deepened as His
human nature became more open to the experience. St. Luke
speaks of it very simply: "Jesus increased . . . in favor with
God." Growth in holiness takes place on a much broader scale

than growth in knowledge. Jesus, as a man, experienced growth in knowledge chiefly through the relationship which grew with Yahweh as His Father.

## In Wisdom and Knowledge

St. Luke makes it very clear that Jesus grew in knowledge. To be more accurate, Jesus grew in wisdom. Jesus did grow in various areas of human knowledge and skills. He learned the carpenter's trade from Joseph. He learned the art of cooking from His mother, Mary. But the area in which Jesus especially grew, because of His great concern about it, was His understanding of the Holy Scriptures. These were the writings of the Old Testament: the Law, the Prophets, and the Wisdom books. The knowledge of God's Word in the Scriptures was wisdom for the Jews. It gave Him a share in God's own thought and plan of love for mankind's salvation.

This process of the growth of Jesus is easy to discern. He learned to read from Mary and Joseph. He then must have spent many hours poring over the Scriptures. At the age of twelve He was in the Temple *asking questions*. How He must have wondered as He read the sacred books! Did He perhaps stop to ask Mary the questions that plagued Him? If so, her answers must have been simple, direct, and deeply enlightened, reflecting her own openness to the Spirit. She would have spoken from a rich and deep spiritual experience, for she had carefully pondered the Word in her heart.

Jesus also gained knowledge of the Word from others. Sabbath after Sabbath He listened to rabbis preach on the Word in the synagogue. Year after year He made the pilgrimages to the Holy City on the great feasts, especially that of Passover. But this knowledge was not mere intellectual growth. It was primarily a growth in understanding the Word *as given by* the Spirit. Jesus spoke from personal experience when later He promised the Spirit to His apostles. He assured them the Spirit would lead them into the complete truth (Jn. 16:13). He "will teach you everything and remind you of all I have said to you" (Jn. 14:26). The mystery of the action of the Spirit through His various gifts and charisms upon the precious humanity of Jesus is indeed the mystery of Jesus as the Christ. The mystery of the growth of Jesus in wisdom is the mystery of the Spirit of Truth, bringing Jesus to a comprehension of Yahweh's plan as revealed in His Word.

## Messianic Identity

Every book of Scripture held the interest of Jesus. He researched every theme of Scripture from its beginnings to its manifold implications. But one area of the Holy Word surely held a special fascination for Him. He searched for all those passages in the Law, the Prophets, and the Psalms which spoke of the Messiah to come. The promise of the Messiah is the heart of the Old Testament. The Old Testament history of salvation grew into a body of literature as the promise of a Savior was reiterated through the ages. The Spirit of Truth had to bring Jesus to an accurate comprehension of these messianic passages.

Was there a moment, maybe on some Sabbath in the synagogue or at home in Nazareth, when He began to realize that He was the One of whom the prophets and holy authors spoke? How did He react to such a realization? The Scriptures are silent on the matter. But since He was a "man like us in all things but sin," did He not react much as we would react? Perhaps He spent days in an unusual spirit of quiet. His mood may have become more pensive. Maybe He asked various people to pray with and for Him. Without doubt He became increasingly aware of the Spirit speaking to Him, revealing to Him the truth, revealing to Him His deepest self.

There is one fact free of any conjecture: When Jesus fully realized He was the Messiah of whom the Scriptures spoke, He was faced with an awesome decision. He knew He should follow the way of the Messiah as the Spirit revealed it to Him. Jesus was free, truly free. He made the decision freely under the action of the Spirit. It changed His life. He must have shared the decision

with His mother. They must have talked over the matter for
hours. But as they pondered, prayed, and shared, the answer became clearer. What He would have to do became clearer. His
life at Nazareth was over. The years of preparation were
finished. He would now have to close the carpenter shop, give up
His trade, and leave home. He would have to take to the road.
He would have to place Himself totally under the guidance of
God as His Lord and Father. His decision would affect Mary
drastically. He had a deep concern for her, yet He could not let
her stand in the way. For thirty prayerful years Mary had
watched as He "increased in wisdom, in stature, and in favor
with God and men." Now she understood very well that He had
to be about His Father's affairs. We can see them embrace in
mutual surrender to the plan of their Lord. He walks away. The
Spirit drives Him *away* from Nazareth *to* the banks of the Jordan. The journey took Him to John the Baptizer. A totally new
life was beginning for Him and for her. Both now had to live by
faith in Yahweh, who was saying to them: "I am with you; do
not be afraid."

St. Luke tells us what happened:

> Now when all the people had been baptized and while Jesus after
> his own baptism was at prayer, heaven opened and the Holy
> Spirit descended on him in bodily shape, like a dove. And a voice
> came from heaven, "You are my Son, the Beloved; my favor rests
> on you." [3:21–22.]

Let us consider the baptism of Jesus by John and the Father's
baptism of Jesus in the Spirit. These two baptisms differ greatly
in significance. They are separate, yet joined by prayer.

## Responsibility for All Sin

Why did Jesus receive John's baptism? This baptism was "a
baptism of repentance for the forgiveness of sins" (Lk. 3:3).
Jesus was sinless; He had no sins of His own to be forgiven. But
there were the sins of mankind, of every man and woman since

Adam and Eve. These were the sins for which He received the baptism of John, "a baptism of repentance for the forgiveness of sins." The moment Jesus knew in the light of the Spirit that He was the Messiah of whom the Old Testament spoke, at that moment He knew He had to make His own the sins of all mankind. He had to assume responsibility before Yahweh and before all mankind for the expiation of those sins. He had to atone for them; He had to win forgiveness for mankind's guilt of sin. There was no other way for Him to be Savior. So when He left Nazareth, He went straight to John. That was why the Spirit raised up John and gave him the baptism of repentance, so Jesus could receive it as the sinner in our place! The decision Jesus had made privately somewhere was the decision He now made publicly while being baptized. It was His official acceptance of, and commitment to, the messianic work of salvation.

What a heavy and awesome moment! True, Jesus Himself was sinless. But at that moment He had *all* sin placed on His heart and on His shoulders. Luke tells us He prayed *after* He was baptized by John. Was this moment unlike that in the Garden of Olives when He pleaded with the Father to let the chalice pass Him by? Was it not similar to the moment on the Cross when He cried out to His Father, "Why have you deserted me?" We sinners can scarcely bear the weight of our own sins, much less those of anyone else. Jesus bore the weight for all sinners:

> Ours were the sufferings he bore,
> ours the sorrows he carried. . . .
> he was pierced through for our faults,
> crushed for our sins.
>
> [Is. 53:4-5.]

Was this not one of those times when Jesus "offered up prayer and entreaty, aloud and in silent tears" (Heb. 5:7)? Was this not one of the occasions when Jesus needed to pray? He felt deeply His inadequacy in the face of the task He had taken on. He sensed His need of Yahweh, of His Father's love and help. How He must have cried out to His Father for the wisdom and the strength needed even to begin the task!

## A Prayer Heard

The Father answered that prayer immediately. In fulfillment of all the messianic prophecies, a few of which we quoted above, the Father poured out His messianic Spirit in fullness upon Jesus. "The Holy Spirit descended on him in bodily shape, like a dove" (Lk. 3:22). At this moment Jesus *in a unique way* became the Christ or Messiah—that is, the Anointed One of Yahweh. Jesus sensed the effect of the ever-deepening action of the Spirit upon His humanity. There had been many in Old Testament times who had in a similar way received an anointing: the judges, the prophets, especially the kings as they ascended the throne of David. But the anointing of Jesus was different. The fullness of the anointing in which He received the Spirit is shown by the Evangelists throughout their Gospels. John says of Jesus, "He whom God has sent speaks God's own words: God gives him the spirit without reserve" (Jn. 3:34).

The Father spoke to Jesus as He filled Him with His Spirit. "You are my Son, the Beloved; my favor rests on you" (Lk. 3:22). The Father had spoken many times already to Jesus through His Spirit. He would do so even more frequently in the future. But it was very important for the Father to speak to Him *now,* and for Him to say to Jesus what He did. The baptism by John was into the anguish of personal responsibility for the sins of humankind. Jesus, overcome by this anguish and crying out for help needed the strengthening power of Yahweh's Spirit. He needed the comforting solace of the Father's reassuring love. Jesus, the man, not "incapable of feeling our weaknesses with us" (Heb. 4:15), needed to know God would be with Him in His mission. What God had told Moses, "I shall be with you," He also told Jesus.

But now the words of reassurance and divine companionship could be expressed in terms of divine paternity: "You are my Son." Jesus truly was His Son; He was the Son of God Incarnate. Now through the gift of the Spirit Jesus in His manhood was

being lifted up more fully into the experience of His filial relationship with God as Father. God who was always His Father
was now experienced as Father by Jesus as man. This happened
through the action of the divine Spirit in a way that would
henceforth sustain Jesus in all His trials. What this newly experienced filial relationship meant to Jesus is described in the Gospel
of John. John states Jesus was always turning to His filial relationship with the Father *as the justification for everything He
said and did!* The action of the Spirit in this relationship was
ever experienced by Jesus.

Jesus is the Christ because He has been given the Spirit in
messianic fullness. Jesus *lives* as the Christ by surrendering in
His humanity totally to the enlightening and empowering action
of this messianic Spirit which He now possesses. Thus do the
Evangelists picture the life of Jesus. Luke especially notes:

> Filled with the Holy Spirit, Jesus left the Jordan and was led by
> the Spirit through the wilderness. [4:1.]

There follows the Evangelist's description of the temptations.
Then later he adds:

> Jesus, with the power of the Spirit in him, returned to Galilee,
> and his reputation spread throughout the countryside. He taught
> in their synagogues and everyone praised him. [4:14.]

## His First Homily

Luke then quotes the first homily Jesus preached in the synagogue at Nazareth. In giving us *this* homily Luke obviously
wants us to know what the consciousness of Jesus was as He
began His public ministry. It was the consciousness He had received from the Father, the fullness of His Spirit at the Jordan.
Now He knew He was truly the Christ, the Messiah, in
fulfillment of the Old Testament prophetic utterances. Luke
describes the scene for us:

> He came to Nazara, where he had been brought up, and went
> into the synagogue on the Sabbath day as he usually did. He

stood up to read, and they handed him the scroll of the prophet Isaiah. Unrolling the scroll he found the place where it is written:

> The spirit of the Lord has been given to me,
> for he has anointed me.
> He has sent me to bring the good news to the poor,
> to proclaim liberty to captives
> and to the blind new sight
> to set the downtrodden free,
> to proclaim the Lord's year of favor.

He then rolled up the scroll, gave it back to the assistant and sat down. And all eyes in the synagogue were fixed on him. Then he began to speak to them, "This text is being fulfilled today even as you listen." [4:16–20.]

We have already noticed that, for Luke, what characterized Jesus most during His first thirty years was the element of growth. We can safely assume the bestowal of the messianic Spirit upon Him by the Father effected a rather profound interior transformation. Jesus, in the synagogue at Nazareth, was a man very sure of Himself. He knows who He is and what His mission is. This is a different man from the one bent in prayer just after He was baptized by John and immersed in the sins of mankind.

This transfiguration had been the work of the Spirit. Jesus had been made aware of His Christship, His messianic mission. This awareness had not come easily to Jesus. The Spirit had not let Him take an easy road to the maturity of self-identity: He had to suffer the agony of the forty days' retreat in the desert to arrive at that maturity.

The significance of these forty days is easily understood if we see them in the light of the Israelites' sojourn of forty years in the desert. Those were years during which Yahweh brought His people to the realization that they could really trust him. They learned that He meant what He had said, "I shall be a God caring for all your needs." During the forty days Jesus experienced many trials and temptations. He had to learn His Father's idea of the Christ, the Messiah.

The three temptations are ways in which Satan attempted to get Jesus to live out His role as Messiah in a manner contrary to His Father's wishes. But Jesus could not be the Messiah on His own terms; He had to be the Messiah on terms laid down by His Father. The Spirit had to inform Jesus what these terms were and give Him the strength to be faithful to them. To be the Christ means to be obedient to God in the light and power of His Spirit. The Spirit has to be a Spirit of truth, revealing the mind of the Father. He has to be the Spirit of love and power, the Spirit of total obedience to the Word of the Lord.

## In the Power of the Spirit

A number of ideas had been circulated as to what the Messiah should be like. As Jesus came to a new maturity during His forty-day retreat, He learned the Father's idea of the Messiah. He was to be a man of Yahweh's Spirit. This meant the *gifts* of the Spirit (Is. 11:2), the *fruits* of the Spirit (Ga. 5:22), and the *charisms* of the Spirit (1 Co. 12:8–11) all had to be present in Him. They had to be manifest in His behavior.

The gifts directed Him in His personal relationship with God His Father. John's Gospel describes the intensity, depth, and warmth of this relationship.

The fruits of the spirit control primarily one's relationship with one's fellow man. They are all manifestations of love. That Jesus possessed each of these fruits to perfection is evident on every page of the Gospels. So perfect was He in love that He made it His new commandment: "love . . . as I have loved" (Jn. 15:12).

The charisms are graces of power and extraordinary knowledge. Their purpose is to equip one with power and knowledge to be of service to persons in need. Now Jesus came to accomplish the difficult work of man's greatest need, salvation. Jesus had to perform that work as a man in the power of God. The manifestation in Jesus of the Spirit's gifts of knowledge and

power point Him out to all men as the Christ. It was thus that
Isaiah described Him:

> Courage! Do not be afraid.
> Look, your God is coming . . .
> he is coming to save you.
> Then the eyes of the blind shall be opened,
> the ears of the deaf unsealed,
> then the lame shall leap like a deer
> and the tongues of the dumb sing for joy.
> [35:4–6.]

John the Baptist in prison received reports of the results showing how Christ used these gifts of the Spirit. So he sent two of
his disciples to Jesus with the question, "Are you the one who is
to come, or must we wait for someone else?" (Lk. 7:19). In answer, Jesus first

> cured many people of diseases and afflictions and of evil spirits,
> and gave the gift of sight to many who were blind. Then he gave
> the messengers their answer, "Go back and tell John what you
> have seen and heard: the blind see again, the lame walk, lepers
> are cleansed, and the deaf hear, the dead are raised to life, the
> Good News is proclaimed to the poor and happy is the man who
> does not lose faith in me." [Lk. 7:21–23.]

As Jesus gave this summary of His apostolate to the messen-
gers, He was very much aware of the Spirit's knowledge and
power working in Himself. He knew that through the charisms
of the Spirit He heard and understood His Father. He knew at
every moment what the Father wanted Him to do. He understood the Old Testament and He preached the Word of the
Lord. He read the hearts of the people, and knew by what spirit
each one talked or acted. He prophesied about future events. He
could cure the sick, drive out evil spirits, and work miracles.
Jesus was fully aware that these messianic signs were being realized in Him through the power of the Spirit. By this power the
Kingdom of God was indeed being established through Him:

> If it is through the Spirit of God that I cast devils out, then know
> that the Kingdom of God has overtaken you. [Mt. 12:28.]

According to Mark, after Jesus had worked many signs and wonders and had cured a blind man, He took His apostles aside to Caesarea Philippi:

> On the way he put this question to his disciples, "Who do people say I am?" And they told him. "John the Baptist," they said, "others Elijah; others again, one of the prophets." "But you," he asked, "who do you say I am?" Peter spoke up and said to him, "You are the Christ." [8:27–29.]

## The Anointed of the Lord

"You are the Christ." Belief in this assertion about Jesus has to be an integral part of our faith in Him. There is much scriptural evidence in both Testaments that deals not with the divinity but with the messianic or Spirit-anointed character of the Savior. We cannot know the real Jesus if we do not know His humanity.

We are to know He was a man like us in all things but sin. We are to know that this man emptied Himself of divine glory in order to become a slave. We are to know He was anointed by the Spirit in fullness and thus became the Christ or the Messiah. This will forever set Him apart from other men. For Him to have been conceived by Mary through the overshadowing power of the Spirit, for Him to have lived His human life with every thought and action dictated by the Spirit of God: these things make Him the Chosen One of God, the Son of Man, the Holy One—in a word, the Christ.

To know what it means for Jesus to be the Christ helps us not only to understand Him but also to understand the Christian life. Life can be Christian only when it is a life *in the Spirit* as was the life of Jesus. There would be little opposition to the charismatic renewal if believers in Jesus *understood* what they say when they call Jesus the Christ. The charismatic renewal celebrates the gift of the fullness of the Spirit to Christians. This gift is theirs because they believe Jesus is the Christ and because they follow him as Lord. How can one be called *Christian* if one is not anointed by the Spirit of God? How can one be anointed by the Spirit of God if one's life does not manifest His gifts, His fruits, His charisms? Acts 11:26 tells us, "It was at Antioch that the disciples were first called 'Christians.'" The same gifts and charisms of the Spirit were being manifested in their life as in the life of Jesus. If He could be called the Christ, they could be called Christians. Jesus became the Christ when the Father gave Him His Spirit in fullness. So a community of believers becomes fully Christian when Jesus bestows on it this same Spirit in fullness.

Not merely to call Jesus the Christ but to know more fully what is meant when one calls Him the Christ—this must be one of the objectives of the current renewal of the Church. This knowledge must grow in every Christian community if Christians are to live, as the Christ did, "in the Spirit."

Yes, the title *Christ* has indeed taken on a new meaning for me. I now know that we can never understand the name of Jesus until we as Christians experience in our life those same anointings "in the Spirit" as did the Christ.

# CHAPTER V

# Jesus Is Lord

"Do you believe in Jesus Christ, God's only Son, our Lord . . . ?" I was asked this question not long after I was born. It was asked before I was "born again" by water and the Holy Spirit in the sacrament of Baptism. Through my godparents at that baptismal birth I answered firmly that I do believe in Jesus Christ.

Each of us in the sacrament of Baptism has made this same profession of faith in Jesus. We have repeated it many times in our lives. Every time we say the great doxology, the conclusion to any official prayer in the Roman Liturgy, we renew that profession of faith made in Baptism. This doxology is addressed to God as our Father "through Jesus Christ, Your Son, our Lord, who lives and reigns with You in the Holy Spirit, God, forever and ever."

This frequently made profession of faith uses four names for our divine Savior. These names are of special importance in expressing the Christian faith. Otherwise, they would not be included in this most ancient and constantly used doxology of liturgical prayer.

*Jesus* is the first name mentioned in this prayer. The Father Himself instructed Mary at the Annunciation to so name their Son, who would be born of her through the power of the Spirit. *Jesus* means "Yahweh saves." This is the name that best fits Him as "a man like us in all things but sin."

The doxology continues, "Through Jesus Christ. . . ." *Christ* is more a title than a name. Jesus was conceived by Mary through the power of the Holy Spirit. Jesus grew up in all areas of human development through the unique action of the Spirit upon His humanity. Jesus can rightly be called "the Christ" after the time of His conception. Nevertheless, this is the title that was most appropriate to Him when He received the anointing of the Holy Spirit in messianic fullness on the banks of the Jordan. Then He became the Christ and the Messiah of the Lord. Then it was that the prophecies regarding Him as the Messiah were uniquely fulfilled. The title *Christ* is to be affirmed of Jesus in a special way during His public ministry. But the title suited Him even more when He had risen from the dead. Now in His risen glory the certainty of His anointing by the Spirit of Yahweh is affirmed.

This Jesus, son of Mary, also is proclaimed to be Christ, "the Son of God," in this prayer. He is the Word made flesh. He is the Incarnate Son of the Father. "Son of God" is the name proper to Jesus inasmuch as He is a divine person, the second person of the adorable Trinity.

The doxology prayer next speaks of this Jesus as "our Lord." What does it mean to proclaim Jesus as Lord? It is to this mystery of the Lordship of Jesus that we now turn our attention.

### The Lord as Man

In treating of the Lordship of Jesus, we are still considering the *humanity* of Jesus. As a divine person or the Son of God, Jesus, of course, is Lord. As Son of God, He shares fully the life and work of the Father. And the Father is Lord. Indeed, *Lord* is the Father's own name. As we saw earlier, the Hebrew name *Yahweh* was rendered as *Kyrios* in the Greek, which in turn is *Lord* in English. Under the name Yahweh, Lord, as we saw earlier, God revealed Himself to Moses, and through Moses to all of us:

"I shall be with you. . . . I Am who I Am. . . . I Am. . . . This is my name for all time; by this name I shall be invoked for all generations to come." [Ex. 3:11, 14–15.]

We speak of Jesus as "our Lord." We do so because of the authority and power over the Church and all creation that He obtained through His Resurrection. There is nothing startling about calling Jesus "Lord" because He is a divine person. The completely incomprehensible truth of the Christian faith is that the *man* Jesus, raised from the dead, deserves to be called "Lord"!

In so calling Jesus "our Lord," we are not denying in any way His divinity. That divinity is implicitly acknowledged when we proclaim the *man* risen from the dead as "our Lord." For in no sense could Jesus *become* Lord by rising from the dead if He were not the Son of God sharing, as Son of the Eternal Father, His Lordship. Yet when we proclaim Jesus as "our Lord," we say more than that He is God. We assert that He, as the man who died on the cross for our sins, rose from the dead. And through this rising from the dead, He came mysteriously into possession of the rights, powers, and prerogatives of God as Lord.

It was the Father who told Mary to call His Son, conceived of her, Jesus. And the title *Christ* became His at His anointing by the Spirit on the banks of the Jordan. In a similar fashion the Father gave a new name, that of *Lord*, to Jesus, His Son, the moment He rose from the grave. Both titles, *Christ* and *Lord*, could have been used of Jesus before His Resurrection. The Evangelists do give the title *Lord* to Jesus during His public ministry, even though this does not happen very often. Jesus could even then, as man, be called Lord. This was because of His unique power over life and death, which He had through His possession of the messianic Spirit.

Because Jesus shared in the Spirit in *messianic fullness*, He could participate in His Father's Lordship over all creation. Through this same fullness of the Spirit the Father gave Jesus authority to represent Him in a way no other prophet had been able to do. Yet Jesus as the Christ possessd the Spirit only in a measure. This is especially true when the comparison is made with His possession of the Spirit in His glorified condition as risen Savior. For in His Resurrection the Father gave Jesus His Spirit not merely in a messianic fullness but in what we can only call a divine and infinite fullness. What is the difference between these two "fullnesses"?

## A New, Immortal Life

The difference is evident in the condition of His human nature before and after His Resurrection. Before His Resurrection Jesus is truly a man like us. He is mortal. He is weak. He can suffer and die. But after His Resurrection Jesus is immortal. He can no longer die! He is risen—not to this life, as was Lazarus, who had to die again; Jesus is risen to a totally new life, one in which He cannot die! Death has no more power over Him. There is a difference then in Jesus, the man, having the Spirit in messianic fullness and in His having that same Spirit in divine fullness. The one makes Jesus the Christ or Messiah; the other truly makes Him Lord.

On His Resurrection day, then, Jesus truly experienced a new birth. On that day the Father gave Him a new name. An early Christian hymn, recorded by Paul, states this very clearly:

> But God raised him high
> and gave him the name
> which is above all other names
> so that *all beings*
> in the heavens, on earth and in the underworld,
> *should bend the knee* at the name of Jesus
> and that every tongue should acclaim
> Jesus Christ as Lord,
> to the glory of God the Father.
>
> [Ph. 2:9–11.]

There is no name greater than the name *Lord*. We have seen the reason for this: *Lord* is God's own name. But this is now the name the Father gives to Jesus! He gave it to Him on the day of His Resurrection. Jesus was named Lord because of what happened to Him in His risen humanity. Through that act of divine power in which He was raised from death into the glory of the Godhead Jesus became Lord with the Father.

The above hymn makes it clear that because He is called Lord, Jesus has a right to the adoration of the entire universe, and of all mankind. Jesus, the man, in His risen glory, has been "raised high" above all creation. Jesus, the man, raised from the dead, now possesses unquestioned and unlimited sovereignty!

## Faith, the Work of the Spirit

The Gospels reveal that the people, even the apostles, had great difficulty in believing Jesus was the Christ. The New Testament writings do not give us any evidence that they had a similar difficulty in coming to faith in His Lordship. This amazes us. The Lordship of Jesus is a much greater mystery than His Messiahship! The answer lies in the Spirit given by Jesus on Pentecost. It is the work of the Pentecostal Spirit to impart the gift of faith in the Lordship of Jesus! That Spirit had not yet been given in messianic fullness before the first Pentecost except to Jesus Himself, and perhaps to His Mother, Mary. And so we read about the faith struggles of the disciples. What a faith expansion they experienced once Jesus had given His Spirit!

> For this reason the whole House of Israel can be certain that God has made this Jesus whom you crucified both Lord and Christ. [Ac. 2:36.]

And St. Paul says very confidently:

> No one can say, "Jesus is Lord," unless he is under the influence of the Holy Spirit. [1 Co. 12:3.]

All this is but a fulfillment of the promise Jesus made about the Spirit!

> When the Advocate comes,
> whom I shall send to you from the Father,
> the Spirit of truth who issues from the Father,
> he will be my witness.
>
> [Jn. 15:26.]

The Spirit bears witness to Jesus and brings people to true faith in Him, to the faith He is not only the Christ but also our Lord.

Faith in the Lordship of Jesus implies much more than faith in His Messiahship. The followers of Christ experienced a great *expansion* of faith on the first Pentecost. In Chapter II we examined a similar development of growth in faith, one recorded in the Old Testament. In ancient times people considered their gods to be territorial deities. The Israelites likewise considered Yahweh to be uniquely *their* God, the One who ruled over *them* in their land.

The deportation into Babylonian Exile was a traumatic experience for them. In being moved to a foreign land, they felt that their God, Yahweh, had abandoned them. The Exile taught them, through the prophets, that the gods of the other nations were not really deities at all. They were powerless "nothings." Yahweh, on the other hand, was the only God, the only true God. As such, He had to be God not merely over the small country of Judah but over all creation. Furthermore, He was God over all peoples, even over their captors. What an expansion of faith for them! What good news!

Yahweh expanded the faith of His people by letting them realize He was Lord not only of the Israelites but of all nations. He brought about this expansion of faith by the "agony, passion, and death" of the Babylonian Exile. Through the Exile the followers of Yahweh were awakened to a new life, a new realization that Yahweh, their Lord, always with them, was with all other peoples as well.

So, too, did Yahweh bring Jesus through the agony, passion, and death so that, through His Resurrection, He could become with Him Lord of the universe. But Yahweh, through the agony of Jesus, also brought His followers through an Abraham-test of their faith. They saw the One whom they had come to know as the Christ suffer and die. But then He rose gloriously from the grave. Thus was Jesus manifested as Lord through the glory of His risen presence and power. And Yahweh brought the followers of Jesus through the agony of doubt and confusion owing to His death. He brought them to the light and strength of faith in His Lordship as Risen Savior.

This test of faith, a journey into the faith that Jesus is Lord, is evident in the case of the two disciples on their way to Emmaus. They were downcast because their faith in their "great prophet" had been shattered. In answer to the question of Jesus, "What things?" they were astonished that this stranger did not know of their predicament. They poured out their story to Him as they walked along. The story revealed they were suffering an Abraham-test of their faith:

> "Our own hope had been that he would be the one to set Israel free. And this is not all: two whole days have gone by since it all happened; and some women from our group have astounded us: they went to the tomb in the early morning, and when they did not find the body, they came back to tell us they had seen a vision of angels who declared he was alive. Some of our friends went to the tomb and found everything exactly as the women had reported, but of him they saw nothing."
>
> Then he said to them, "You foolish men! So slow to believe the full message of the prophets! Was it not ordained that the Christ should suffer and so enter into his glory?" [Lk. 24:21–26.]

## Difficulties in Believing

Undoubtedly these two disciples in this faith-experience represent the whole community of believers. What an awakening this was for all the first followers of Christ! Note that it was not the appearance of the Risen Christ that brought them to a new life of faith, nor the reports of those who "had seen and believed." Luke tells us:

> When the women returned from the tomb they told all this to the Eleven and to all the others. The women were Mary of Magdala, Joanna, and Mary the mother of James. The other women with them also told the apostles, but this story of theirs seemed pure nonsense, and they did not believe them. [24:9–11.]

The two disciples of Emmaus, too, came back to the apostles and disciples to relate their story. Luke again says:

> They were still talking about all this when he [Jesus] himself stood among them and said to them, "Peace be with you!" In a state of alarm and fright, they thought they were seeing a ghost. But he said, "Why are you so agitated, and why are these doubts rising in your hearts? Look at my hands and feet; yes, it is I indeed." [24:36–39.]

Mark, in reporting the same story tells us that Jesus even rebuked them for their lack of faith:

> Lastly, he showed himself to the Eleven themselves while they were at table. He reproached them for their incredulity and obstinacy, because they had refused to believe those who had seen him after he had risen. [16:14.]

Only gradually during the forty days after Easter did they come to accept the fact Jesus had truly risen from the dead. They did not as yet see Him, even though risen from the dead, as Lord and God. This was to be the witness of the Spirit whom Jesus Himself was to give. And when that Spirit came, He brought, instantaneously it would seem, the interior certitude that Jesus had indeed, through His Resurrection, become Lord. That was why Peter could conclude his homily on Pentecost Day in this way:

> ". . . the whole House of Israel can be certain that God has made this Jesus whom you crucified both Lord and Christ." [Ac. 2:36.]

What an expansion of faith the disciples of Jesus had undergone! In this new faith they too experienced a *resurrection!* They began to live a totally new life, a life in Jesus as the Christ and the Lord.

In a sense Jesus earned His Lordship. As Incarnate Son of God He could have come into the world in a glorified condition. However, He emptied Himself of this glory so that He could

> . . . assume the condition of a slave,
> and become as men are;
> and being as all men are,

he was humbler yet,
even to accepting death,
death on a cross.

[Ph. 2:7–8.]

## The Father's Gift

This does not deny the fact that the Lordship of Jesus was the Father's gift to Him. The Father rewarded Jesus for His loving obedience, His heroic faith, and His total openness to the Spirit. The New Testament usually attributes the work of the Resurrection of Jesus from the dead to the *Father.* "God raised this man Jesus to life" (Ac. 2:32). "But God raised him high" (Ph. 2:9). "God the Father . . . raised Jesus from the dead" (Ga. 1:2). The Resurrection is the Father's gift to Jesus, His Incarnate Son. It was the Father who *made* Jesus *Lord* in raising Him from the dead. Jesus knew beforehand the Father was going to do this. It was for this glorification He had prayed:

"Father, the hour has come:
glorify your Son,
so that your Son may glorify you. . . .
Now, Father, it is time for you to glorify me
with that glory I had with you
before ever the world was."

[Jn. 17:1, 5.]

Jesus was given the assurance by the Father, through His Spirit, that this glorification would take place:

As soon as Judas had taken the piece of bread he went
out. Night had fallen.
    When he had gone Jesus said:

"Now has the Son of Man been glorified,
and in him God has been glorified.
If God has been glorified in him,
God will in turn glorify him in himself,
and will glorify him very soon."

[Jn. 13:30–32.]

The Risen Christ is a *human being*. In possessing a new and glorious life, He is not less a human being, but more so. There are no words to describe how Jesus felt on Easter morning. The mind of no human person can fathom what His thoughts were. How great must have been His gratitude to the Father for the gift of the Resurrection, and for the Lordship status that went with it! How humble yet how joyful Jesus must have felt when He heard the Father call Him by the name of LORD! At that moment the whole history of salvation must have passed quickly before the mind of Jesus. With the Father He now, too, was revealing Himself as Lord to Moses, Joshua, Jeremiah, and all of His people: "I shall be with you" for "I Am who I Am."

Jesus is Lord. He became Lord through His Resurrection from the dead. This is clearly stated by Paul in the opening verses of his letter to the Romans:

> From Paul . . . specially chosen to preach the Good News that God promised long ago through his prophets in the scriptures. [1:1-2.]

And what is this "Good News"?

> This news is about the Son of God who, according to the human nature he took, was a descendant of David: it is about Jesus Christ our Lord who, in the order of the spirit, the spirit of holiness that was in him, was proclaimed Son of God in all his power through his resurrection from the dead. [Rm. 1:3-4.]

We note how this text is built around the four names proper to our Savior: Jesus, the Christ, Son of God, our Lord! Jesus is the name proper to Him, who, "according to the human nature he took, was a descendant of David." This Jesus is the one who became the Christ "in the order of the spirit, the spirit of holiness that was in him" because that Spirit was given Him in messianic fullness. But this Jesus Christ, in this same "order of the spirit, the spirit of holiness that was in him," was proclaimed Son of God in all His power through His Resurrection from the dead.

This text also calls Jesus our Lord. The Christship and the Lordship of Jesus are both mysteries that belong to the same order, the order of the Holy Spirit within Him. They are both mysteries of the Spirit in and upon His *human nature*. The difference is that in His Christship Jesus received the Spirit only in messianic fullness. In His Lordship, however, He received this same Spirit in divine or infinite fullness. Another difference is that in His Christship He was proclaimed Son of God only in some of the power that was proper to him in that relationship. In His Lordship, however, He could be proclaimed Son of God lacking none of the power due to Him. In being conceived of Mary under the power of the Holy Spirit, He became one of us. Thus, Jesus in His human nature bore the condition of a slave. But in His Resurrection Jesus received back all that He had given up. The Resurrection was a true homecoming for Jesus. That day He came back home to His Father!

What does it mean for the man Jesus to be proclaimed Son of God in all the power proper to Him in that status? It means that He is Lord. It means that everything God is as Yahweh, the Risen Jesus now is. It means that He is a God-with-us, that He has chosen people in order to live with them. It means that He is God who abides with these chosen people to share with them the fullness of His life as God. It means that Jesus, the Risen Christ, is the full revelation and manifestation of God as Yahweh. He is now the One who says, "I am He who is always with you."

## I Am with You

The mystery of the Lordship of Jesus brings to fulfillment the essential revelation of God as Yahweh given throughout the Old Testament. The risen man Jesus was personally aware of this. The "I-am-with-you" is clearly present in everything Jesus says on the occasion of His post-Resurrection appearances.

Repeatedly Yahweh had told His chosen ones: "I am with you; therefore, do not be afraid." Jesus repeats this exhortation, making it His own:

> And there, coming to meet them [the women], was Jesus. "Greetings," he said. And the women came up to him and, falling down before him, clasped his feet. Then Jesus said to them, "Do not be afraid." [Mt. 28:9–10.]

Yahweh, because He claimed to be a God-with-them, promised His people His care and protection. But He asked His people to trust Him. Jesus makes the same request:

> "Do not let your hearts be troubled.
> Trust in God still, and trust in me."
> [Jn. 14:1.]

It is because Jesus, as Risen Savior, is now Lord that He can take away all fear, worry, and anxiety. Because He is in the total control of every situation without violating in any way the free will of His creatures. As Lord, He can bestow peace of heart and mind and cause us to feel secure. As the Father gave Jesus the name Lord on Easter morning, so is peace His Easter wish and gift to everyone. This is that peace which the world cannot give, which He alone can and does give:

> Jesus came and stood among them. He said to them, "Peace be with you," and showed them his hands and his side. The disciples were filled with joy when they saw the Lord, and he said to them again, "Peace be with you." [Jn. 20:19–21.]

During the forty days following His Resurrection Jesus often gave evidence that He was aware of His Lordship. The Evangelist Matthew is a most powerful witness to this awareness of Jesus, the Risen Savior, that He is Yahweh. The *last* thing he has Jesus say to His apostles before His Ascension, and likewise, the last sentence of His Gospel is: "And know that I am with you always; yes, to the end of time" (Mt. 28:20).

From this discussion we know that the Lordship of Jesus refers to the mystery of the human nature of Jesus possessing all the power and wisdom of the Godhead through the possession in infinite fullness of the Holy Spirit. The early Christians knew the Lordship of Jesus was the central mystery of the Christian faith. We can understand why their earliest and best creedal formula was the succinct "Jesus is Lord!" In proclaiming Jesus to be Lord they knew they were implicitly professing faith in all the dimensions of His being, especially in His Christship and in His divinity.

We have examined the relationship of the Christship of Jesus to His Lordship. But what is the relationship of His Lordship to His divine personality? To believe Jesus is Lord is not yet saying explicitly that He is a divine person. But the man Jesus could never have become either Christ or, much less, Lord, if He were not the Son of God. Faith in the divinity of Jesus is included in our profession of faith both that Jesus is Christ and that Jesus is Lord. Why is this so?

## Related Mysteries

If Jesus had been only a human person, He could not have received the Spirit sufficiently to make Him either Christ or the Lord. Man as a person is open to, and capable of, receiving the divine life through the gift of the Spirit. Philosophers and theologians term this an "obediential power" in man. There are many levels of being among creatures. Man is an animal and possesses a unique level of being. No other animals are persons. They cannot receive into themelves the very life of God through the gift of His Spirit. They do not have this obediential power. They do not have the capacity to be divinized through the gift of the Spirit. But people do have this capacity, for they are personal beings.

But, great as is this power and dignity of man, it has limits. A human person, though able to receive the Spirit, can receive Him only with limitation. The fullness of the Spirit that human persons receive is a fullness that lets them indeed be called Christians, but only Christians. No human person, not even Mary, is able to receive the Spirit in such a measure as to become a Christ.

This is why the divinity of Jesus is so fundamental to the mysteries of His Christship and His Lordship. The man Jesus is not a human but a divine person. His divinity confers upon His human nature that power which no other human being can have. Jesus alone has the power to receive the Spirit of God in such a measure as to make Him be the Christ. That fullness of the Spirit which makes Him be the Christ is properly called messianic.

This measure of the Spirit enables Him to be the Messiah or the Christ. But to call Jesus the Christ is already implicitly to call Him God. For Jesus could not be the Christ if He were not a divine person.

The obediential power which the divinity of Jesus confers upon His human nature is therefore unlimited. The human nature of Jesus is able to receive the Spirit in a fullness that makes Him be not only the Christ but even Lord! It is in His Resurrection that Jesus received the Spirit in such measure! The Risen Jesus is now able to do everything that His Father as Lord can do. Though the man Jesus is doing everything now, He cannot do it of Himself as man. All is given Him by the Father. The Father gifted Him with the Lordship through the gift of the Spirit in infinite fullness in His Resurrection.

What was true of Jesus as the Christ here on earth is even more true of Him now that He is Lord:

> I tell you most solemnly,
> the Son can do nothing by himself;
> he can do only what he sees the Father doing:
> and whatever the Father does the Son does too.
> For the Father loves the Son
> and shows him everything he does himself,
> and he will show him even greater things than these,
> works that will astonish you.
>                                    [Jn. 5:19–20.]

We, too, can receive the very life of God, the Spirit. An obediential power renders us also capable of divinization. We possess the divine life to the degree that the Spirit lives in us. Though this power to receive the Spirit is present in every human person, no one has it in a sufficient degree to become the Christ or the Lord. The only human nature with the capacity to receive the Spirit of God so as to become Christ and Lord is that of Jesus.

It follows that Jesus must be true God as well as true man. Jesus, the true man, because He was also true God, could as man become the Christ. Through His Resurrection from the dead He could also become Lord. The Christship and the Lordship and the divinity of Jesus are distinct aspects of His person. Yet they are deeply interrelated. Jesus had to bring His apostles first to faith in His Christship. The Spirit then used the Christship of Jesus on Pentecost Day to build a firm faith in His Lordship. The relationship between the Lordship and the divinity of Jesus is particularly intimate. The New Testament confirms that faith in the Lordship of Jesus brought the early Christians to faith in His divinity.

The early Christians expressed this faith very succinctly. We have this expression of faith in the doxology to the official prayers of the Church. These prayers are addressed to God, our Father, "through Jesus Christ, Your Son and our Lord." As Son, Jesus is brought into relationship with God His Father. As Lord, Jesus is brought into relationship with us. He is our Lord.

The Father has made Him Lord for our sakes, so that He could be a more effective Savior for us. If only we could understand this new source of life given us in His Lordship. If only we could let Him be Lord in our lives. Then we would have, as when we are in love, a life of unending surprises and continuous fresh starts.

Proudly we call Him "our Lord." *Our* Lord He is, the Lord of all of us. He belongs to us. But He asks us to submit to Him in utter openness, and therefore in utter completeness. That is the heart of the Christian life: a life of faith and trust in Jesus, our Lord!

# CHAPTER VI

# The Lord
# Is Our Savior

We have already seen that Jesus, our Savior, risen from the dead, is the Lord of our lives. This is the central mystery of the Christian faith. Jesus, the Risen Christ, is the full revelation and manifestation of God as Yahweh, as Lord, as "I am He who is always with you." So profound, so all-encompassing is this mystery of the Lordship of Jesus that we are drawn to meditate upon it further. Yes, Jesus is Lord! But how did He become Lord? What does His Lordship mean to us? In simplest terms the answers to these questions are: (1) He saved us; (2) we are saved.

The way Jesus became Lord leads us directly into the salvific character of His life and death. Jesus became Lord through His work of saving us from our sin. And who is the Lord? Our Lord is none other than Jesus of Nazareth, the man

> born of a woman, born a subject of the Law, to redeem the subjects of the Law and to enable us to be adopted as sons. [Ga. 4:4–5.]

Our Lord is none other than the man who, while He lived on earth, was a "man like us in all things but sin" (Eucharistic Prayer IV). Our Lord is the Christ, the man who fulfilled His mission in the wisdom and power of the Spirit. He is now our Lord only because He has saved us.

It is true, God sent his word to the people of Israel, and it was to them that *the good news of peace was brought* by Jesus Christ— but Jesus Christ is Lord of all men. You must have heard about the recent happenings in Judaea; about Jesus of Nazareth and how he began in Galilee, after John had been preaching baptism. *God had anointed him with the Holy Spirit* and with power, and because God was with him, Jesus went about doing good and curing all who had fallen into the power of the devil. [Ac. 10:36–38.]

Our Lord is none other than Jesus, the Christ, who lived His life in obedience and love. He thought not of asserting His own righteousness. In every act of His humanity He thought only of bringing about our salvation. Can we possibly envision this Jesus, the Christ, having thus given Himself to redeem us, as not obtaining over us the rights of Lordship, the privileges of being God-with-us? He not only gifted us with His human presence, but gave it to the point of death. Through conquering death He rose to a new life of presence with us, that of being Lord. Jesus, in a word, is truly the One who has saved us. He brought to fulfillment that work of redemption and salvation which God as Lord began and promised throughout the Old Testament.

But this salvation is now no longer a promise. It is an accomplished fact. The evidence of its accomplishment is the Lordship of Jesus. In answer to our first question, "How did Jesus become Lord?" we simply affirm that He became Lord by His saving act. This man Jesus, anointed by the Spirit, has absolute Lordship over us because He saved us by purchasing us with His blood.

The second question, "What does the Lordship of Jesus mean to us?" has validity only because Jesus *has* saved us. He is our Lord inasmuch as He has fulfilled the work of our salvation. He belongs to us because His Lordship is totally salvific in purpose and character. This is why we call Him *our* Lord. However, we must never forget that His Lordship over us flows from His relationship to God as Father. Sonship expresses this relationship of Jesus to God. Jesus is Son to God His Father. He is God's Son but He is our Lord. As Lord He belongs to us. The Father has given Him to save us and to bring us to fullness of Life. He is Lord for our sake. Indeed He became Lord for our sake.

## Yahweh Is Savior

Already in the Old Testament we find affirmation of the truth that God as Lord is a God who saves us. God is Yahweh, God with His people, only because He is always at work saving. Deutero-Isaiah confirms this truth of Yahweh's saving power:

> Do not be afraid, for I have redeemed you;
> I have called you by your name, you are mine.
> Should you pass through the sea, I will be with you;
> or through rivers, they will not swallow you up.
> Should you walk through fire, you will not be scorched
> and the flames will not burn you.
> For I am Yahweh, your God,
> the Holy One of Israel, your savior.
>
> [43:1, 3.]

As Deutero-Isaiah spoke these words, he could look back over more than a thousand years of salvation history. God had always been with His people. This prophet knew his God to be Lord because he experienced His presence always at work saving. Deutero-Isaiah knew that this God had deigned to reveal His name, Yahweh, Lord, to Moses. But more than that, He had chosen Moses for a saving mission. Moses was to lead God's people out of Egyptian slavery into the Promised Land. God's name and nature were revealed not so much in the words Moses heard but in the mission on which he was sent.

Little by little, and step by patient step, God revealed Himself as Yahweh, as saving Lord. He saved His people from temporal and physical calamities, from famine, pestilence, and defeat in battle. And always it was to prepare them for a deeper faith in His nearness to them and a greater hope in future blessings.

## The Exodus, the Type of Salvation

Yahweh's call of the patriarchs was but the historical preparation for the saving event of the Exodus. The Exodus included

not only the departure from Egypt and the deliverance from
slavery. It also included the journey to Mount Sinai and the giving of the Law. It included the making of the Covenant, the
journey through the desert, and finally the entrance under
Joshua into the Promised Land. It was in and through this
unified series of events that God manifested Himself as Yahweh,
Lord, as a God who saves. He had assured Moses that this would
happen:

> "I shall be with you . . . and this is the sign by which you shall
> know that it is I who have sent you . . . After you have led the
> people out of Egypt, you are to offer worship to God on this
> mountain." [Ex. 3:11–12.]

God kept His word. The Exodus imprinted itself indelibly on
the faith-consciousness of Israel. It was the greatest of all the
saving acts of Yahweh. The chosen people had pondered in faith
its religious significance. It became for them the *type* of all God's
saving acts for His people.

Referring to the Exodus as a type means conferring on it a
special character, certain implications. The expression "type"
refers to a special meaning given to some biblical passages. Be-
sides their literal sense, there is another way in which these passages are to be understood. They point to a future reality in the
history of salvation. They are signs of this future reality. These
things, facts, or persons become a figure or type of the reality to
come.

The use of the type or typical sense as opposed to the literal
sense does not rest on conjecture by scholars or Bible readers. An
event in the Bible used as a type is based on the divine
authorship of the Scriptures. God uses a type to show the unity
of salvation history. He shows in this way that all His revelations
and salvific actions have a continuity. His designs *are* worked out
through history. A type is the promise of the future fulfillment of
God's saving plan.

The Exodus became the type of all the ways Yahweh saves His
people. The Israelites came to understand the Exodus not only as
a figure of what God had done, but as a type of what He would

continue to do. Yahweh spoke through His great prophet, Moses. Thus the Israelites came to know the real significance of Exodus:

> Put this question, then, to the ages that are past, that went before you, from the time God created man on earth: Was there ever a word so majestic, from one end of heaven to the other? Was anything ever heard? Did ever a people hear the voice of the living God speaking from the heart of the fire, as you heard it, and remain alive? Has any god ventured to take to himself one nation from the midst of another by ordeals, signs, wonders, war with mighty hand and outstretched arm, by fearsome terrors—all this that Yahweh your God did for you before your eyes in Egypt?
>
> This he showed you so that you might know that Yahweh is God indeed and that there is no other. He lets you hear his voice out of heaven for your instruction; on earth he lets you see his great fire, and from the heart of the fire you heard his word. Because he loved your fathers and chose their descendants after them, he brought you out of Egypt, openly showing his presence and his great power, driving out in front of you nations greater and more powerful than yourself, and brought you into their land to give it you for your heritage, as it is still today.
>
> Understand this today, therefore, and take it to heart: Yahweh is God indeed, in heaven above as on earth beneath, he and no other. [Dt. 4:32–39.]

God revealed himself as Lord through the saving act of the Exodus. And so God revealed Himself as a Lord who saves through the Exodus. Thus did His people come to know Him as a Lord, as a God who, being Lord, was intent on saving them. Mankind had sinned, but they knew God to be with them to save them from their sin.

## The Passover Meal

Not only did the people of the Exodus learn to know God as Lord and Savior. Through the Passover Meal the meaning of the Exodus and the Convenant was renewed annually in a liturgical rite. Through this liturgy the Exodus Covenant was re-enacted.

The people of each generation were thus brought into the experience that their Yahweh was a God indeed. He was their only God, a God who loved them, who had chosen them to be His. Because He loved them, He was in the process of always saving them. At the end of his life, Moses recalled for the Israelites the significance of both the Exodus and the Covenant:

> "Not with you alone do I make this covenant today and pronounce these sanctions, but with him also who is not here today as well as with him who stands with us here in the presence of Yahweh our God." [Dt. 29:13–14.]

Joshua, similarly, at the end of his life renewed the Covenant with the people of his day:

> That day Joshua made a covenant for the people; he laid down a statute and ordinance for them at Shechem. . . . Then Joshua sent the people away, and each returned to his own inheritance. [Jos. 24:25, 28.]

The Psalter reveals also how deeply the Savior character of the Lord Yahweh was impressed on the faith-consciousness of the Israelites. The following passages from the Psalms (Grail Translation) confirm this:

> The man with clean hands and pure heart . . .
> shall receive blessings from the Lord
> and reward from the God who saves him.
>                          [Ps. 23(24):4–5.]

> To you, O Lord, I lift up my soul. . . .
> Make me walk in your truth, and teach me:
> for you are God my savior.
>                          [Ps. 24(25):1,5.]

> You keep your pledge with wonders, O God our savior,
> the hope of all the earth and of far distant isles.
>                          [Ps. 64(65):5.]

> O God, our savior, come to our help, come for
> the sake of the glory of your name.
> O Lord, our God, forgive us our sins.
>                          [Ps. 78(79):9.]

Come, ring out our joy to the Lord;
hail the rock who saves us.
[Ps. 94(95):1.]

As we have seen, the Exodus is the type of all salvation. That is why Deutero-Isaiah saw the return from Babylonian Exile in terms of the first Exodus:

Thus says Yahweh,
who made a way through the sea,
a path in the great waters;
who put chariots and horse in the field
and a powerful army,
which lay there never to rise again,
snuffed out, put out like a wick:

No need to recall the past,
no need to think about what was done before.
See, I am doing a new deed,
even now it comes to light; can you not see it?
Yes, I am making a road in the wilderness,
paths in the wilds.

The wild beasts will honor me,
jackals and ostriches.
because I am putting water in the wilderness . . .
to give my chosen people drink.
The people I have formed for myself
will sing my praises.
[Is. 43:16–21.]

Here is another of many scriptural passages that sing of Yahweh as Savior:

Sing a new song to the Lord
for he has worked wonders.
His right hand and his holy arm
have brought salvation.

The Lord has made known his salvation;
has shown his justice to the nations.
He has remembered his truth and love
for the house of Israel.

All the ends of the earth have seen
the salvation of our God.
Shout to the Lord all the earth,
ring out your joy.

Sing psalms to the Lord with the harp—
with the sound of music.
With trumpets and the sound of the horn
acclaim the King, the Lord.
    [Ps. 97(98):1–6, Grail Translation.]

Throughout the Old Testament, then, God reveals Himself as a Lord who saves His people. He does this by showing He is in their midst in order to share His life with them. The Old Testament thus helps us to understand the Lordship of Jesus. For the role of Jesus as Savior is inextricably bound to His title of Lord. His Lordship is the perfection of His salvific work.

The first Exodus was essentially a work of salvation. It saved the people from being doomed for time-without-end to Egyptian slavery. The first Exodus became the type of every phase of God's plan for saving us. The return from Exile was thought of as a Second Exodus. Likewise, the Evangelists saw the saving work of Jesus in terms of this ancient type.

## The Exodus of Jesus

In the first Exodus the chosen people passed from a condition of slavery into a new life in the Promised Land. Jesus emptied Himself of glory and became a slave like all men. But then He passed from this sinful human condition, through suffering and death, into the glory of the Resurrection. He received sovereignty from the Father at His Ascension. Was not this passage of Jesus an Exodus, another Passover? John has stated this insight most clearly:

It was before the festival of the Passover, and Jesus knew that the hour had come for him to pass from this world to the Father. . . . Jesus knew that the Father had put everything into his hands, and that he had come from God and was returning to God. [13:1, 3.]

The passage of Jesus through this world to the Father by means of His Passion, Death, Resurrection, and Ascension is not just another Exodus. It is not just another Passover. It is *the* exodus, *the* Passover, the one that fulfills all the others. God did not save His people by means of the first Exodus. Neither did He do so by means of the exiles' return to the Holy Land. God *did* save His people by the Death and Resurrection of Jesus.

The saving character of the Lordship of Jesus is very distinct from the saving quality of the Lordship of Yahweh in the Old Testament. This distinct quality is defined as that of definitive accomplishment. Worthy of all praise are Yahweh's signs and wonders in the Old Testament. But they did not effect our salvation. The Old Testament merely foreshadowed the salvation to come in Christ Jesus.

Yahweh's signs and wonders were all a type of the Exodus, the Passover, of Jesus. The argument of the author of the letter to the Hebrews can become ours. The reality is in Christ Jesus our Lord. Only the Passover of Jesus has that distinct quality of definitive accomplishment. We need not look beyond it for forgiveness of our sins and for re-establishment of communion with God. We can place all our faith in Jesus, for we know He *has* saved us by His Death and Resurrection:

It is not as though Christ had entered a man-made sanctuary which was only modeled on the real one; but it was heaven itself, so that he could appear in the actual presence of God on our behalf. And he does not have to offer himself again and again like the high priest going into the sanctuary year after year with the blood that is not his own, or else he would have had to suffer over and over again since the world began. Instead of that, he has made his appearance once and for all, now at the end of the last age, to do away with sin by sacrificing himself. Since men only die once, and after that comes judgment, so Christ, too, offers himself only once *to take the faults of many on himself,* and when he appears a second time, it will not be to deal with sin but to reward with salvation those who are waiting for him. [Heb. 9:24–28.]

Indeed, Jesus the Lord has effected our salvation. Faith in that Lordship has a distinct quality. This quality is that of absolute *power*. The New Testament insists that power belongs to faith in Jesus because He is Lord. For example:

I tell you most solemnly,
whoever believes in me
will perform the same works as I do myself,
he will perform even greater works,
because I am going to the Father.
Whatever you ask for in my name I will do,
so that the Father may be glorified in the Son.
If you ask anything in my name,
I will do it.
[Jn. 14:12–14.]

To ask "in the name" of Jesus is to ask in His name as Lord, for He became Lord by going to the Father. St. Paul has this prayer of petition in his letter to the Ephesians:

May the God of our Lord Jesus Christ, the Father of glory, give you a spirit of wisdom and perception of what is revealed, to bring you to full knowledge of him. May he enlighten the eyes of your mind so that you can see . . . how infinitely great is the power that he has exercised for us believers. This you can tell from the strength of his power at work in Christ, when he used it to raise him from the dead and to make him sit at his right hand, in heaven. . . . *He has put all things under his feet,* and made him, as the ruler of everything, the head of the Church; which is his body, the fullness of him who fills the whole creation. [1:17–23.]

Note that it is not necessarily the faith itself which is strong, though it may be. Faith becomes powerful because it allows God to act in the life of the believer. Indeed, the power with which God can work is proportionate to the power He displayed in

making Jesus Lord of the universe and head of the Church. In
Paul's letter to the Ephesians, the thought is expressed in the
doxology which concludes his second prayer:

> Glory be to him whose power, working in us [believers], can do
> infinitely more than we can ask or imagine; glory be to him from
> generation to generation in the Church and in Christ Jesus for
> ever and ever. Amen. [3:20–21.]

Finally, St. John writes in his First Letter:

> Who can overcome the world?
> Only the man who believes that Jesus is the Son of God,
> Jesus Christ who came by water and blood . . .
> with the Spirit as another witness.
>
>                                          [5:5–6.]

Why is faith in the Lordship of Jesus so powerful? Because
through such faith in Him Jesus is free to share with the believer
the fullness of salvation.

What does the Lordship of Jesus mean to us? It means we are
all saved. It means that we share the absolute power of His
Lordship. It means that we have absolute power over everything
evil and that everything good is ours. The Father has entrusted
everything to the Lordship of Jesus, and He shares everything
with us. He is our Lord. His Lordship is ours. The fruits of His
victory are twofold in the character. They include a share in the
victory that Jesus has won over the forces of evil which held creation in bondage till the moment He died, and a share in the life
of the Spirit.

## Victory with Jesus

These forces of evil can be grouped into four categories: Satan
and his legions of evil spirits; sin, especially the guilt of sin,
which estranges us from God; sickness of body, soul, and mind,
which is the consequence of sin upon our nature; and finally,
death, physical death, the separation of soul and body which ter-

minates our life here on earth. Jesus has won a complete victory over all these powers of evil.

We do not always see the victory of Jesus over sickness and death. Such vision may have to wait until a future time, even until the Last Day. But Jesus as Lord has won the victory. Moreover, He has it only so that He can share it eventually and completely with us. The totality of this victory is best illustrated by death. It is usually held that we will rise from the dead only on the Last Day. Yet this is no longer a cause for sorrow. Jesus reassures us:

> "I am the resurrection.
> If anyone believes in me, even though he dies, he will live,
> and whoever lives and believes in me will never die."
>
> [Jn. 11:25–26.]

St. Paul proclaims the meaning of the Resurrection of Jesus for the Christian by exclaiming:

> *Death, where is your victory? Death, where is your sting?*
>
> [1 Co. 15:55.]

He can only add:

> Let us thank God for giving us the victory through our Lord Jesus Christ. [1 Co. 15:57.]

The victory of Jesus over death is complete. Not only will we rise from the dead, but through death we enter into greater and fuller life. We are then more alive in Christ. We are more present not only to Him but to our loved ones on earth. Death truly loses its sting. Death itself dies, is put to death.

### Fullness of Life

There is yet another way to share in the full fruits of the salvific work of Jesus. His work was not limited to conquest of the enemies of life—namely, Satan, sin, sickness, and death. This negative phase of the work of salvation was accomplished in view of a more positive saving work. Jesus also saved us by bringing us into communion with Yahweh. He does this by sharing the Spirit of Yahweh with us. Jesus, through His Death and Resurrection, received the Spirit of Yahweh in order to give us that Spirit. In this gift of the Spirit especially lies the salvific work of Jesus.

The "gift of the Spirit" signifies not only those graces through which we share in the victory of Jesus over Satan, sin, sickness, and death. It also signifies all those graces and blessings through which we share in the very life of God. Through these graces we enter into communion with the Father. The presence of the Spirit within us calls for the eventual glorification of our bodies. But until then His work in us is one of purification and sanctification.

The Christian life is entirely, from the beginning to the very end, a living in the Spirit of Jesus. Each grace and divine blessing has its source in that Spirit given us by Jesus as Lord. The Spirit within us is the greatest of all His gifts. The Spirit is the source of all His other graces. The Spirit is, as Jesus Himself has said, a fountain of living waters within us springing up to eternal life (Jn. 4:14).

As we grow in faith and surrender to Jesus as Lord, our hearts are open more fully to the action of this Spirit through His many gifts and blessings. There is a point at which we are said to have received a fullness of the Spirit. This fullness is usually characterized by the "abundant life" we begin to live. It is a life characterized by the manifestation of many of His fruits and charisms.

For it is Jesus who gives all life, all divine life, from the initial grace of faith to that of ultimate glory in Him. All this work of sanctification and glorification is the work of the Spirit of Jesus. Jesus can give His Spirit to sanctify and glorify us only because He has become Lord. There is no end to the spiritual gifts and blessings Jesus, our Lord, desires to give so we can truly come to life. And Jesus as Savior never stops calling us to this fullness of

new life. Hence, Paul begins the great hymn which opens his
letter to the Ephesians:

> Blessed be God the Father of our Lord Jesus Christ,
> who has blessed us with all the spiritual blessings of heaven in
>     Christ.
>
> [1:3.]

Jesus said it more simply:

> "I have come
>     so that they may have life
>     and have it to the full."
>             [Jn. 10:10.]

Such is the twofold salvific work of Jesus. He saves us from
evil. He fills us with His Spirit. In virtue of this work of salvation
He has become our Lord. He is our Lord as Savior. And He is
truly our Savior because He is now Lord.

It is important to remember the salvific character of the
Lordship of Jesus. As fearful creatures we tend to stress His authority and power, and this tends to make Him be for us an un-
feeling tyrant, a kind of absentee landlord. It is true that Jesus as
Lord is the master of all creation. The sun, moon, and stars and
all the forces of nature must now obey Him. But He will never
exercise His power except out of love for us. We can be at ease
in the face of His Lordship. He acts only for our good. He loves
us so deeply that He will not spare us suffering and pain. But
His will is always *good* toward us. As Lord, He remains a Good
Shepherd. He leads each of us out of Egyptian slavery and is
with us on the way to the Promised Land. As Lord and Savior
He is with us all the way!

# CHAPTER VII

# The Gift
of the Spirit

To speak about Jesus as our Savior in any meaningful way is to speak of His gift of the Spirit. Scripture unites the two so intimately that the mention of one implies the other. Jesus became Lord through His Resurrection and Ascension. But according to Scripture Jesus did not manifest this fact to His followers until He sent the Holy Spirit. Indeed, the followers of Jesus came to a faith awareness that He was Lord only when they experienced the Holy Spirit as His gift and as the Promise of the Father. The fact that Jesus was able to send the Spirit from the Father was witness to them that He had indeed become Lord. Peter's realization of this fact is powerfully expressed in the final sentences of his homily on the first Pentecost:

> "God raised this man Jesus to life, and all of us are witnesses to that. Now raised to the heights by God's right hand, he has received from the Father the Holy Spirit, who was promised, and what you see and hear is the outpouring of that Spirit. . . . For this reason the whole house of Israel can be certain that God has made this Jesus whom you crucified both Lord and Christ." [Ac. 2:32–33, 36.]

This chapter will further explore how Jesus exercises His Saviorship, His Lordship, as we journey forward seeking to share in the *fullness* of His saving power.

## A Spirit of Wisdom

Yes, they *saw* and *heard* "the outpouring of that Spirit." The Spirit poured out upon them manifested His presence in what they saw and heard and felt. The Spirit's presence was humanly experienced. This *experience* of the Spirit *was the gift of Jesus*. It brought the apostles and disciples to the faith that Jesus was Lord.

In general this experience was one of *wisdom* and *knowledge*. Through these gifts the apostles understood what the Scriptures had said about this Spirit. We hear Peter, for example, filled with wisdom and knowledge, quoting Joel 3:1–5 in his homily. They also understood what Jesus Himself had said about this Spirit. On Pentecost Sunday when they felt the movement of the Spirit among them they surely recalled the last meal Jesus had with them here on earth. He had spoken pointedly and frequently then about the Spirit. They realized now that Jesus was then trying to show them the connection between His glorification and the Spirit He would send. Otherwise, He would not have talked so much about the Spirit during His final night with them. Their eyes of faith were opened, indeed, through their experience of the Spirit on Pentecost Sunday.

## A Spirit of Power

But the experience of the Spirit was not only one of wisdom and knowledge. It was also one of *power*. All kinds of signs and wonders began to take place. The followers of Jesus had a totally new courage in proclaiming the mystery of Christ. They prayed and spoke in the gift of tongues and in foreign languages. There were healings and miracles. But their most powerful experience of the Spirit was the *faith* it produced in the Lordship of Jesus. Greater than wisdom and knowledge, greater than the healings and wonders was this new gift of faith. In their experience of the Spirit an undying faith in the Lordship of Jesus was born. Now they were able to turn back to what Yahweh had said in the

Scriptures and to what Jesus had said. They could accept it all with greater meaning and deeper understanding.

In this chapter I want to search the Scriptures with you. Yahweh has said much in them about His Spirit. Scripture does attest to the fact that the gift of the fullness of the Spirit is one which Jesus can give only because He in His risen glory has become Lord.

On that first Pentecost Day Peter quoted the prophecy of Joel because he was convinced it had come to fulfillment. Peter understood that the Spirit which Jesus gave that day was the fulfillment of that prophecy.

"After this
I will pour out my spirit on all mankind,
Your sons and daughters shall prophesy,
your old men shall dream dreams,
and your young men see visions.
Even on the slaves, men and women,
will I pour out my spirit in those days.
I will display portents in heaven and on earth,
blood and fire and columns of smoke."

The sun will be turned into darkness,
and the moon into blood,
before the day of Yahweh dawns,
that great and terrible day.
All who call on the name of Yahweh will be saved.
[Jl. 3:1–5.]

This is an accurate description of the first Pentecost spoken by the prophet four hundred years before it became a reality. Without doubt Joel was asked to explain this prophecy as he had uttered it. How might he have explained it?

## Yahweh's Agent

The Spirit holds a unique place in God's dealings with mankind. Christians, especially in recent centuries, have had difficulty understanding the work of the Spirit in the Church and the world. This is in part because we have lost the Jewish concept of the work of the Spirit. A contemporary Catholic biblical scholar, John L. McKenzie, in a summary of his study of the Spirit in the Old Testament, has indicated that everything Yahweh does outside Himself He does through His Spirit.[1] The implications of this statement are vast. The whole of creation is a manifestation of the creative power of the Spirit of Yahweh. Through the Spirit Yahweh brought all things into being. In the Spirit all things "live and move and are." The Spirit as the breath of God is the breath of life in all things that exist.

What is true of creation is also true of God's plan for salvation. By means of His Spirit Yahweh fulfills His plan to save His people. The Spirit is Yahweh's agent accomplishing the Father's saving will without in any way violating our freedom. He is the Spirit within salvation history. Yahweh's Spirit is at work saving, whether it be in the heart of the individual, in people influencing us, or in the events of history.

Even more importantly, the Spirit is Yahweh's liaison between Himself and us. It is through His Spirit that Yahweh communicates His will to us. It is through that same Spirit that we hear the word of Yahweh and have the power to obey Him. The whole of what we know as salvation history, from the call of Abraham on, is the work and manifestation of the Spirit of Yahweh. Even when Scripture does not explicitly attribute something to the Spirit of Yahweh, it is He who is at work, if it is part of Yahweh's plan.

In the light of this, the Spirit of Yahweh is at work in *little* things as well as in *great*. The Spirit can be present in ways so small that they are hardly discernible even by a person of great faith. Again, the Spirit can be so manifestly present that we wonder why all people do not readily acknowledge His presence and action. The distinction between the hardly discernible and the evident manifestations of the Spirit is of great importance in

[1] John L. McKenzie, "Aspects of Old Testament Thought," *The Jerome Biblical Commentary*, ed. Raymond E. Brown, S.S., et al. (Englewood Cliffs, N.J.: Prentice-Hall, Inc., 1968), pp. 742–43.

discussing the Spirit that Jesus, the Lord, has given to His Church. There is a tendency to limit the action of the Spirit to the more manifest and extraordinary. As a result, the more subtle and gentle activity of the Spirit in the Christian life is over-looked, not recognized. On the other hand, there is a similar tendency to deny the need for, or at least the usefulness of, the more extraordinary gifts of the Spirit. Yet Scripture asserts that to speak of the Spirit as having been given in messianic fullness is to speak of Him as present in power.

## The Desire of Moses

An incident in the life of Moses seems to preintone this mes-sianic age of the Spirit spoken of in Joel's prophecy. Moses had become deeply irritated over the people's murmuring. He com-plained bitterly to God over the burdens of his office in being the leader of such a stubborn and stiff-necked people. Yahweh, in answer, told Moses to gather seventy of the elders of Israel and bring them to the Tent of Meeting:

> "Let them stand beside you there. I will come down to speak with you; and I will take some of the spirit which is on you and put it on them. So they will share with you the burden of this na-tion, and you will no longer have to carry it by yourself." [Nb. 11:16–17.]

Moses accordingly

> . . . gathered seventy elders of the people and brought them around the Tent. Yahweh came down in the Cloud. He spoke with him, but took some of the spirit that was on him and put it on the seventy elders. When the spirit came on them they prophesied, but not again. [11:24–25.]

The account continues, however, in this way:

> Two men had stayed back in the camp; one was called Eldad, and the other Medad. The spirit came down on them; though they had not gone to the Tent, their names were enrolled among the

rest. These began to prophesy in the camp. The young man ran
to tell this to Moses. "Look," he said, "Eldad and Medad are
prophesying in the camp." Then said Joshua, the son of Nun, who
had served Moses from his youth, "My Lord Moses, stop them!"
Moses answered him, "Are you jealous on my account? If only
the whole people of Yahweh were prophets, and Yahweh gave his
Spirit to them all!" [11:26–29.]

Joel may have had this text from Numbers in mind as he ut-
tered his prophecy about the Spirit. He knew the Spirit is the
One through whom Yahweh does everything outside of Himself.
He knew Yahweh had guided and empowered Moses as leader
of His people through the Spirit. He could understand why
Moses desired all the Israelites to be filled with this breath of
Yahweh. Moses and his seventy helpers would have had a much
easier time leading God's people if such had been the case.

Joel desired, as did Moses, that *all* the people receive Yahweh's Spirit. And Yahweh spoke of this desire in prophecy
through Joel: The day will come when Yahweh will pour out His
Spirit not merely on *one* man, Moses, not merely on a *few chosen*
assistants, the seventy elders, but upon *all the people!* That will
be the messianic age, the age of the Messiah! The *whole nation*
will possess the various charisms of the Spirit, symbolized and illustrated in the text of Joel by visions, dreams, and prophecies.

These are the three traditional ways in which Yahweh through
His Spirit guided His chosen servants. Through the possession of
these various gifts and charisms of the Spirit, Judah will emerge
an ideal community, something it had never been. The Spirit of
God will revivify this dormant and prostrate Israel. God promises a second and greater creation!

## On All Mankind

To emphasize the fact that Yahweh will pour out His Spirit on
all mankind, Joel singles out those classes of society which mankind is wont to overlook. Society ignored and rejected the old,

the young, slaves, and women. But these are the ones whom Yahweh will favor with the charisms of His Spirit.

Yahweh's favor to the down and out, to His people in slavery in Egypt, will be renewed and repeated. Joel describes the out-pouring of the Spirit by Yahweh in messianic fullness, in terms that recall the first Exodus. That great event of liberation, which reached its climax at Sinai in the Covenant, was marked by wonders, by blood, by fire and smoke. Judah's future delivery, accomplished through the Spirit, will be another Exodus. God's intervention in human affairs, the sending of the messianic Spirit, will shake the cosmos. That Spirit will cast the "deities" of the sun and moon, still worshiped in Joel's time as gods by the pagan nations, into everlasting darkness!

Joel's prophecy highlights three ideas: The Spirit will come in a fullness never before heard of by anyone; He will be poured out upon all the people without exception; and His coming will be manifested by cosmic disturbances.

Joel's prophecy stands in great contrast to the desire of Moses. Moses, in today's terms, was a great charismatic leader. Yahweh had given him His Spirit in great measure. Yet the very nature of the divine dispensation at the time of Moses meant there was a limit to the measure in which he received the Spirit. This is very clearly indicated by the fact that Yahweh did not pour out His Spirit on the seventy elders in separate measures. He took some of the Spirit already given to Moses and shared that measure with the elders.

The Prophet Joel looks forward to "those days" of the Messiah when such limitations in the gift of the Spirit will no longer exist. He speaks of the age when every man, woman, and child will receive his own measure of the Spirit of Yahweh.

This is clearly what happened on the day of Pentecost. Peter had reason to quote the prophecy of Joel and use it as the introduction to his Pentecostal homily. He was aware that everyone present in the Upper Room had received a personal measure of the Spirit. Regardless of age, sex, or position, this measure was so great for each one that it manifested itself in a new way of life. Each one experienced a new life of faith, love, peace and joy, courage, ability to speak, and the power to work miracles. Peter viewed the situation correctly. Jesus had given the Spirit in superabundant measure: There was an overflow of the Spirit and His gifts. The Spirit was manifested through an exuberance and an enthusiasm never before experienced by anyone or by any group of people.

Further consideration needs to be given to a phrase in Peter's homily:

> "What you see and hear is the outpouring of that Spirit." [Ac. 2:33.]

## The Spirit in Flesh

Contemporary Christians may find this phrase hard to understand. We have been taught to identify the Spirit with the immaterial. We assume that the Spirit has little or nothing to do with matter, especially with human flesh. However, just the opposite is true! Yahweh has brought all things into being through His Spirit. Therefore, it is the mission of the Spirit to transfigure all of creation, especially human flesh, with the glory of God. Creation finds its culmination in man, male and female. In mankind the material and the immaterial worlds meet and unite. The Spirit will transfigure the universe through His transfiguration of man, male and female.

The Spirit is meant to change people. The Spirit is meant to move people. The Spirit is meant to endow people with new life and new powers. Just as surely as we can say there is no wind unless we see it in the movement of the branches or hear it whistle through the forest, so surely can we say there is no Spirit of Yahweh in messianic fullness unless His presence is somehow evident. That presence is evident in what we see, hear, and feel. The most Spirit-filled day in Christianity, Pentecost, was also the most "sense-filled"! There is a great truth hidden in the reaction of the unbelieving crowd:

> Everyone was amazed and unable to explain it; they asked one another what it all meant. Some, however, laughed it off. "They have been drinking too much new wine," they said. [Ac. 2:12–13.]

Peter in his rebuttal did not deny or explain away the manner in which the Spirit was acting through the exuberant Christians. He did deny that they were drunk.

> "Make no mistake about this, but listen carefully to what I say. These men are not drunk, as you imagine. . . . On the contrary, this is what the prophet spoke of:
>
> In the days to come—it is the Lord who speaks—
> I will pour out my spirit on all mankind. . . .
>
> [2:14–17a.]

The Lord Yahweh was vouching for the fact that what appeared to some to be behavior manifesting a state of intoxication was actually behavior inspired by His Spirit!

"What you see and hear is the outpouring of the Spirit." The Spirit *can* be present and active and yet hardly discernible to our senses or feelings. However, when there is a question of the Spirit being present in messianic fullness, then His presence and action will be evident in easily discernible ways, in ways proper to the Spirit of Yahweh. These need not be ways suitable to our liking. The Spirit was given by Jesus in a fullness which His Father had never given to mankind before. Therefore, from the day of Pentecost on, the Spirit was to be manifested in patterns of behavior that were entirely new, peculiar to the messianic age. These patterns of behavior are described in the so-called *fruits* of the Spirit (Ga. 5:22) and in the *charisms* (1 Co. 12:4–11).

If these patterns of behavior are not present in a community calling itself Christian, then it cannot claim to possess the fullness of the Spirit in any significant degree. Neither can it claim to be living as fully as it should under the Lordship of

Jesus. Faith in the Lordship of Jesus should lead to His gift of
the Spirit in Pentecostal fullness. Such fullness of the Spirit will
manifest itself in the classical ways of the *Spirit-ual* life. Scripture clearly indicates that such is a necessity for spiritual growth.

## The Spirit in Fullness

Unfortunately, the fact that the Christian and the Christian
community are called to such faith in the Lordship of Jesus is
not generally accepted. But only through such faith can a community be open to His gift of the Spirit in messianic or Pentecostal fullness. Granted, there is a comfort in having life regular and
predictable. Granted, there is the failure to see that the fullness
of the Spirit[2] is manifested more in His fruits than in His
charisms. Yet Scripture amply attests to the fact that the Christian life is to be characterized by fullness. We have this word
from our Lord himself:

> "I have come
> so that they may have life
> and have it to the full."
> [Jn. 10:10.]

In His conversation with the Samaritan woman He promised
this richness of life in the Spirit under the image of living water:

> "Whoever drinks this water
> will get thirsty again;
> but anyone who drinks the water that I shall give

2 In this book I seldom use the phrase "baptism in the Spirit," about which
there is far greater controversy than about "fullness of the Spirit." I perceive
a growing tendency to limit "baptism in the Spirit" to a conversion experience. I am not denying or belittling the importance of such an experience; however, in this book I'm concerned not so much with the
experience that may have brought one into the Spirit as with that mystery
of grace which reflects a life surrendered to Jesus as Lord. This mystery
of grace is characterized by a fullness of life that has its source in Jesus'
gift of the Spirit. The relationship between baptism in the Spirit and fullness of the Spirit will be dealt with at length in another work.

will never be thirsty again:
the water that I shall give
will turn into a spring inside him, welling up to eternal life."
[Jn. 4:13–14.]

If the Spirit is to be like a spring of water to the Christian, the evidence of the overflow should be manifest in the Christian's life. He should be a bubbling spring, not a stagnant pool, and certainly not a dry cistern.

One of the major themes of Paul's letter to the Ephesians is that of fullness. Ephesians is the last of the great Epistles of Paul. By the time he wrote this letter, Paul clearly saw that fullness of power and life characterized Jesus as Lord. Paul knew then that power and life were to be characteristic of His followers:

> The God of our Lord Jesus Christ, the Father of glory . . . *has put all things under his feet,* and made him, as the ruler of everything, the head of the Church; which is his body, *the fullness of him who fills the whole creation.* [Ep. 1:17a, 22–23, second italics added for emphasis.]

This is the dynamic vision Paul has of Jesus. He as Lord, in His risen glory, is busy filling the whole of creation from the fullness that He Himself as Lord possesses. Paul further explains in Ephesians 4 that this fullness does consist in Jesus' gift to the Church of His own Spirit:

> The one who rose higher than all the heavens to fill all things is none other than the one who descended. And to some, his gift was that they should be apostles; to some, prophets; to some, evangelists; to some, pastors and teachers; so that the saints together make a unity in the work of service, building up the body of Christ. In this way we are all to come to unity in our faith and in our knowledge of the Son of God, until we become the perfect Man, fully mature with the fullness of Christ himself. [4:10–13.]

In 3:19 also Paul prays that Christians may be "filled with the utter fullness of God." The context clearly shows this to be a fullness of the Spirit of love.

John also uses the theme of fullness throughout his Gospel. This idea is given expression already in his Prologue:

> The Word was made flesh,
> he lived among us,
> and we saw his glory,
> the glory that is his as the only Son of the Father,
> full of grace and truth. . . .
> Indeed, from his fullness we have, all of us, received—
> yes, grace in return for grace.
>
> [1:14, 16.]

## The Eucharist

This fullness of life is so essential to the Christian life that we ask to receive it through Holy Communion.

> "The bread that I shall give
> is my flesh, for the life of the world. . . .
> Anyone who does eat my flesh and drink my blood
> has eternal life,
> and I shall raise him up on the last day."
>
> [Jn. 6:51, 54.]

The Church is so convinced Jesus has placed *all* life into the Eucharist that she boldly expects to receive the fullness of divine graces and blessings through the Holy Meal: "As we receive from this altar the sacred body and blood of your Son, let us be filled with every grace and blessing" (Eucharistic Prayer I).

Jesus could not give the Spirit until He was glorified. But once He came to glory, He gave that Spirit to us. The Spirit, therefore, is also *the* gift of Jesus to the one who eats His flesh and drinks His blood. Moreover, we pray that this Spirit given in fullness will be the source of those best gifts of unity, peace, and love. Luke, in Acts, pictures the Spirit creating the Christian community in a unity of faith and love.

The Eucharistic Prayers picture the Spirit, given anew in fullness through Holy Communion, creating the unity of the Body of Christ which is the Church. "May all of us who share in the body and blood of Christ be brought together in unity by the Holy Spirit" (II). "Grant that we, who are nourished by his body and blood, may be filled with his Holy Spirit and become one body, one spirit in Christ" (III). "And that we might live no longer for ourselves but for him, he sent the Holy Spirit from you, Father, as his first gift to those who believe, to complete his work on earth, and bring us the fullness of grace" (IV). "By your Holy Spirit, gather all who share this bread and wine into the one body of Christ, a living sacrifice of praise" (IV).

"Fullness of the Spirit" is a controversial phrase. This is true because it is so rich in meaning. It is good to remember the difference between a possession of this fullness and aspiring to it. This fullness is essential to Christianity. It is the gift of Jesus as Lord. It is the grace of the Eucharist. All catechesis must in one way or another lead up to this grace, for the Christian who does not aspire to the fullness of the Spirit is choosing to live a life comparable to that in a desert instead of in the Promised Land.

But we are meant to live in the land of promise. The first Eucharistic Prayer begs that we be filled "with every grace and blessing." We accept the Blessed Virgin as being "full of grace." Paul begins his letter to the Ephesians with a hymn of praise to the "Father of Our Lord Jesus Christ, who has blessed us with all the spiritual blessings of heaven in Christ" (1:3).

Fullness of the Spirit is fullness of the faith. It is the fullness of the faith in the sense of belief, the fullness of faith in the sense of trust, and the fullness of faith in the sense of fidelity.

There is no divine grace or blessing of which the Spirit is not the source. That is why so many of the people in the Gospel According to Luke are simply described as being "filled with the Holy Spirit" as, for example: John the Baptist (Lk. 1:16), Elizabeth (Lk. 1:42), Zechariah (Lk. 1:67), Simeon (Lk. 2:25–27). In Acts 6:5 Luke describes Stephen as "a man full of faith and the Holy Spirit," and Acts 6:8 says of him, "Stephen was filled with grace and power and began to work miracles and great signs among the people." To be filled with grace is to be filled with the Holy Spirit. This fullness of the Spirit is the grace Jesus desires to give to every Christian.

## On All Flesh

Yes, Jesus wishes to give this fullness to every Christian because it is meant for every Christian. The "fullness of the Spirit" is the special grace of the sacrament of Confirmation. Confirmation is one of the sacraments of Christian initiation. Its grace *confirms* and brings the grace of Baptism to a certain fullness or fruition. The sacrament of Baptism confers life and makes one spiritually an infant in the Christian community. But this baptismal life is meant to grow and develop.

The Christian infant should become a child, then an adolescent and a young adult in the Christian community. Finally, the sacrament of Confirmation through its grace of the fullness of the Spirit makes the young Christian a mature Christian adult, one equipped to live for others. In Baptism the Spirit given is the source of life. But in Confirmation the Spirit is the source of power, of a fullness of grace. This power enables the Christian to become a competent and responsible servant of the Body of Christ.

The Spirit is relationship. The Spirit unites Father and Son in the Trinity. The Spirit unites the Father and the man Jesus. The boy Jesus was inspired by the Spirit to cry out "Abba!" to God, His Father. This Spirit, given in fullness, establishes the Christian in a new relationship to Jesus. This is His mission: to bear witness to Jesus (Jn. 15:26). The Spirit imparts such faith and trust and love that Jesus becomes real to the Christian. He is present, alive, and active. The Christian now knows, in an existential experience, that Jesus is truly Lord, that He, therefore, is with him always.

It is at this point that the Christian is able to make a free, personal, and total commitment to Christ. From this point on, the Christian can truly live a life for Christ. The fullness of the Spirit makes the Christian a servant, ready to follow the Lamb wherever He leads. The Spirit makes the Christian *apostolic*.

The doctrine of the fullness of the Spirit is crucial in the formation of Christian community. The future of Christianity depends on the number of Christians who will open their hearts to the great gift Jesus wishes to give, the fullness of His Spirit.

It was to be able to give the Spirit that Jesus lived, suffered, and died. When the Baptist bore witness to Him, he said simply:

> "I have baptized you with water but he will baptize you with the Holy Spirit." [Mk. 1:8.]

It was the gift of the Spirit that was so much on His mind between the Resurrection and the Ascension:

> When he had been at table with them, he had told them not to leave Jerusalem, but to wait there for what the Father had promised. "It is," he had said, "what you have heard me speak about: John baptized with water but you, not many days from now, will be baptized with the Holy Spirit." [Ac. 1:4–5.]

There are many Christians who are indifferent to the gift of the fullness of the Spirit. Or they say, "It is not for me"; "I have no need for it." Yes, we are free to reject Christ's gifts. But in so doing we suffer, the Church suffers, and, most of all, Christ suffers. For thus He is kept from fulfilling the deepest yearning of His heart. He cannot fulfill the reason why He suffered, died, and rose again. If we love Christ, we will give Him the joy of giving us His first and greatest gift, the fullness of His strengthening, refreshing, and consoling Spirit.

# CHAPTER VIII

# Life in the Spirit

Every Christian is called to live in the fullness of the Spirit. Jesus truly wills our baptismal grace to reach its fullest development. The very nature of Baptism calls for growth in our relationship with Jesus. In this growth we sense the need and the desire to ask Jesus to release His Holy Spirit within us. This fullness of the Spirit is the grace of Confirmation and of the Eucharist. The question arises: How is this fullness of the Spirit to manifest itself in Christian life?

It could be said that life in the fullness of the Spirit is marked by the operation of one or more of the classical charisms mentioned by Paul in 1 Corinthians 12. This is a prevalent view. But such a view requires a clear understanding of the nature and purpose of these charisms. Some of these charisms often become manifest in the life of a Christian after the baptism of the Spirit.

Nevertheless, the presence and operation of these charisms do not constitute the *life* to be lived by a Spirit-filled Christian. Their presence and activity is not the primary characteristic of life in the fullness of the Spirit. For the Spirit obligates the recipient of His fullness to live a life that has a clearly defined and *permanent* pattern of behavior. The charisms, however, are transient graces, not permanent possessions. They are bestowed in unique situations for the benefit of others. They are not virtues inspiring habitual ways of life.

Yet their role is not to be ignored. They are tools meant to build up the Church as the Body of Christ. The Church cannot be what Christ desires unless Christians possess these charisms and use them for the purpose intended. They are powers for the *development* of life, not qualities of life itself.

How then does the fullness of the Spirit manifest itself in the life of the Christian? In three qualities: in faith, in love, and in humility or humble service. The Spirit takes the life He has bestowed in Baptism—a life similarly characterized by faith, love, and humility—and deepens it. The Spirit confirms the faith, love, and humility. In thus *confirming* the baptismal life, the Spirit calls the Christian to a mode of life in which these virtues are apparent. This happens because the Spirit empowers the Christian to live by a stronger faith, a more heroic love, and a genuine humility.

How does the Spirit empower us with a stronger faith? The Scriptures recognize three aspects of faith: the virtue of faith, the fruit of faith, and the charism of faith. The word "faith" in the Scriptures is used in various ways. At times, as in 1 Corinthians 12:9, it would seem to be a charism. Most frequently it would seem to be what we have traditionally called the virtue of faith; and, again at times, it would seem to be the fruit of faith, namely, fidelity, faithfulness, or trustfulness, as in Galatians 5:22.

## The Witness of Faith

The *virtue* of faith is the first of the Spirit's gifts. By this grace of faith the word preached about Jesus is accepted. We are able to accept Him as our Savior, the Christ, our Lord, and the Son of God. Through this virtue of faith we are brought into a living union with Jesus in His Death and Resurrection. We become sharers in the salvation He was sent to bring. Therefore, the virtue of faith is a saving faith. Paul speaks of it in his letters, especially in Romans and Galatians. Jesus speaks of this faith in His many dialogues in the Gospel of John.

Second, there is the *fruit* of faith, also called fidelity. This fruit of the Spirit enables one to remain loyal to Jesus and faithful to His Word over the course of time. The virtue of faith always remains the source and the inspiration for the fruit of faith: namely, fidelity. Without the virtue there would never be the fruit, just as there would never be the fruit of the vine, grapes, unless there were the root, stem, and branches. Just as time is needed for the fruit of the grapes to grow and ripen, so time is needed for the fruit of fidelity to appear in the life of the Christian.

Third, there is the *charism* of faith. Paul speaks of this kind of faith in 1 Corinthians 12:9. This kind of faith is a unique grace. It is given at times of special stress when one's faith in Jesus is under attack. During the time of stress or danger the Spirit becomes more present to and active in the Christian by means of the charism of faith. The presence enables the Christian to retain *trust* in Jesus and to remain faithful to Him. Without this unique power, in all likelihood, the Christian would turn away from Jesus.

Jesus manifested this faith often in the course of His life: at the Jordan, in the Garden, on the Cross. But Jesus needed this special power of faith many other times during His life: in the desert, when He was tempted; when the crowd wanted to make Him king; when His hearers could not accept His message about the "bread of life" and "walked no more with Him"; when the Jewish authorities wanted to arrest Him; every time His hostile audience wanted to stone and kill Him; and whenever the Father wanted Him to heal, to cast out devils, to raise a dead man to life. This charism of faith is needed to perfect both the virtue and the fruit of faith. The charism of faith is the gift Christians need in time of persecution. It is the grace given to martyrs. It is the power that makes the believer a faithful Christian.

So we note that the first manifestation of the fullness of the Spirit in the Christian is a deeper and stronger life of faith. By this gift of faith the Spirit brings us into a personal relationship with Jesus and sets us on a new way of life. This initial faith truly marks a new birth. This "birth through the Spirit" was spoken of by Jesus in His conversation with Nicodemus (Jn. 3:5). This image of birth gives us an insight into the saving power of this faith and into the personal relationship with Jesus established by it. It also gives us an insight into what happens when Jesus gives His Spirit in fullness. His Spirit deepens, strengthens, and perfects the gift of faith for us. That same Spirit deepens and strengthens the relationship of the Christian to Jesus. The Christian becomes committed and empowered to live for Jesus as the only Lord of his life.

## Finding the Word Anew

There are many ways in which this new faith in Jesus expresses itself. These expressions of faith are experienced by Christians once they have received the fullness of the Spirit. There is usually a new love and hunger for and understanding of Scripture. St. Paul tells us faith comes to us on the occasion of hearing God's Word. Faith is an acceptance of the Word preached about Jesus. The new faith given by the Spirit speaks to the Christian about Jesus his Lord. Often, after the baptism in the Spirit, a person will read Scripture for hours. Scripture reading and meditation on the Word become a regular, even daily, practice.

The Spirit not only creates a hunger for the bread of the Word, but imparts a deep appreciation and an understanding of the message in the Word. People who have never read the Scriptures soon become familiar with the library of books contained in the Bible. They become increasingly familiar with its content. In addition, people develop a facility in remembering what they have read. They ask the most penetrating questions about Scripture or make observations that seem to be Spirit-inspired. The words of Jesus about the Spirit take on a literal fulfillment:

"The Advocate, the Holy Spirit,
whom the Father will send in My Name,

will teach you everything,
and remind you of all I have said to you."
[Jn. 14:26.]

Scripture reading often becomes the *personal word* of the
Lord Jesus for the reader. Jesus through His Spirit will lead the
Christian in some inexplainable way to a text which then stands
out with boldness from the page or which resounds and echoes
deeply in the Christian's heart. It is like the experience of the
two disciples on the way to Emmaus:

"Did not our hearts burn within us as he talked to us on the road
and explained the scriptures to us?" [Lk. 24:32.]

Spirit-filled Christians, open to the operation of His gifts,
truly search the Scriptures for the will of the Lord, for a word of
encouragement or direction. Their expectations are not left un-
fulfilled. Again and again Jesus will speak His Word anew as a
text in Scripture becomes for them the bearer of the mind of
Jesus through the interior action of His Spirit of truth.

## New Dedication to Prayer

This new faith, rooted in a new attention to His Word, also
expresses itself in a new dedication to prayer. The gift of tongues
which is often given when the Christian receives the fullness of
the Spirit, or soon thereafter, accounts partly for this new interest
in prayer. But even those who do not receive tongues seem com-
pelled to pray longer, more fervently and frequently, and certainly more spontaneously.

The Spirit makes Jesus as Lord become real and alive. There is
a compulsion of the Spirit to "spend time with the Lord," to listen to His heartbeat of love, to hear His word, to praise Him for
His goodness, to lay before Him one's needs and petitions. The
fullness of the Spirit often marks a turning point in the Christian's prayer life. Previously prayer demanded effort. One prayed
sporadically, with inefficacy and seeming failure. Now prayer
takes on a new life and power. It is often enjoyable. It is a pow-

erfully fruitful time of communion with Jesus. Above all, it becomes a necessity. One can no longer live without prayer! Fidelity to prayer becomes one of the surest signs that the Spirit has indeed come in fullness.

This new faith is expressed even more certainly in daily life. It takes the form of trust in love and guidance of the Lord Jesus. This trust begets total surrender to Him in the events of daily living. Previously the Christian lived by self-direction. The day was spent manipulating people and situations so as to attain the desires of self-will. Life in the fullness of the Spirit frees one from self, frees one for the will and the work of the Lord. Previously disappointments and failures laid one low. These are now replaced with a new courage and a freedom from fear, a strong spirit of patience and perseverance, a quiet waiting upon the Lord to work in *His* time.

These are some of the expressions of the new faith. In all of our faith expressions this virtue of faith begets the fruit of fidelity. This happens because the Spirit is present with the charism of faith needed by the particular circumstances.

The life of deep faith inspired by the Spirit is evidenced by living examples given us in Scripture. The greatest example of all is Jesus Himself. As we discover the role of the Spirit in His life, we become aware of how deeply Jesus walked by faith and trust. Yes, He did always what pleased the Father. His food was always to do the will of Him who sent Him and to complete His work (Jn. 4:34). But every step into obedience was an act of faith and trust. If Jesus was told beforehand what was going to happen, this did not take away the need for faith and trust. It demanded more faith and more trust.

Mary, too, lived by a deep faith. The faith she displayed at the Annunciation flowed over into her whole life. We are so accustomed to the content of the angel's message to Mary that it no longer startles us. Never before had *any* woman received such a promise: that she would conceive without the agency of male seed! But it was the Lord speaking to her. To His Word she consented even though she did not understand. So much of what happened thereafter to her and to her husband and especially to her Son she did not understand. But Mary believed and trusted. Her faith would have been impossible if she did not have the Spirit in fullness. The faith of Jesus, too, would have been impossible if the Father had not given Him His Spirit in messianic fullness at the Jordan. The kind of faith the Christian ought to have and to manifest is possible only to those who receive the Spirit. Those who have received that Spirit in fullness must authenticate their gift from the Lord Jesus before the world. They do so by the life of faith to which the Spirit calls them.

Fullness in the Spirit is a grace that ennobles and perfects the life to which the Christian is called by Baptism. Therefore, it must manifest itself in a greater life of faith and trust in Jesus as Lord. But for this very reason the second manifestation of the Spirit in fullness has to be that of greater love.

## The Power to Love

When the Spirit comes in fullness, He comes in power. It is this power, the power to love, which the Christian above all needs. There would be no problem accepting the "fullness of the Spirit" if Christians knew how desperately they are in need of divine power. There is no area of human life that so clearly reveals this desperate need as the area of love. Christians throughout the world are not very exemplary in their love for their fellow man. It has been a long time since non-Christians have said about Christians, "Behold how they love one another."[1]

We do not experience a need for the power of the Spirit because we do not truly understand what makes the commandment of Jesus *new:*

> "I give you a new commandment:
> love one another;
> just as I have loved you,

[1] Tertullian, *Apologeticus,* in *Apologetical Works* (New York: Fathers of the Church, Inc., 1950), p. 99.

> you also must love one another.
> By this love you have for one another,
> everyone will know that you are my disciples."
>
> [Jn. 13:34-35.]

What makes this commandment *new?* It obligates us to love one another just as Jesus has loved us. How did He love us? John tells us:

> He had always loved those who were his in the world, but now he showed how perfect his love was. [13:1.]

He proved His love by washing their feet, and then suffering the Passion and death by crucifixion. To love always, to love to the very end, without limit and unconditionally: such was the love of Jesus.

It has been said Jesus loved us as He did because He was God. This kind of thinking lacks an understanding of the humanness of Jesus. It was *as man* that Jesus loved us. It was *as man* that He washed feet and died. But He loved us as He did, even though "a man like us," because He had the power of the Spirit of Love in His heart. That Spirit taught Jesus to love. That Spirit gave Jesus the power to love. Without the Spirit Jesus could not have loved as He did.

Neither can we. The way we have observed the command of Jesus to love has been a scandal to Christians and non-Christians alike. We have failed because we have not had the power to love as we ought. Human love, unassisted by the Spirit, does not have within it the power to love as Jesus has commanded. We must be taught to love and be empowered to love. Only the fullness of the Spirit can bring us this ability.

The Spirit brought this power when He came on Pentecost. The first Christian community was therefore a community of love:

> The whole group of believers was united, heart and soul; no one claimed for his own use anything he had, as everything they owned was held in common. [Ac. 4:32.]

Jesus did not, or could not, expect His disciples to love each other as He loved them until after He was glorified and had sent the Spirit. For this reason Jesus did not promulgate His new commandment until the very end of His life. It was a command which He meant them to observe after He had gone to the Father and sent the Spirit. The context in which Jesus issued His new commandment makes this clear. It was during those heart-rending moments of the Last Supper that Jesus gave His command: Love one another. His beloved Judas had just stepped forth to accomplish the dastardly work of betrayal. In this last conversation with His friends before His Passion Jesus tells them:

> "Now has the Son of Man been glorified,
> and in him God has been glorified.
> If God has been glorified in him,
> God will in turn glorify him in himself,
> and will glorify him very soon."
> [Jn. 13:31–32.]

Jesus has just washed their feet. He knows that in a few moments He will leave the Upper Room for the Garden. He is aware of what pain and anguish will be His during His Passion and death. Yet he knows that He will rise in glory. And then, one with the Father, He will give the Spirit. Thus will He show how perfect is His love for them. In this context of anticipated pain and glory He says, "Love one another, just as I have loved you" (Jn. 13:34).

A life-giving but painful command! What makes this new commandment hard is that, except in isolated situations, it has to be lived out in the framework of some community. It is as members of a community that Christians are to love each other as Jesus has loved them. Yet there seems to be so many failures in the building of Christian community. This is because it is assumed community can be formed without that power to love which comes only with life in the fullness of the Spirit. This is a startling statement to make. But the facts speak for themselves. Where are the truly Christian marriages? Where do we find religious known for the intensity and sacrificial character of their love for one another? Where are the single persons who are truly one with their community?

The new command is to love as Jesus loved. He loved in the power of the Spirit given in messianic fullness. We, too, are to love in the power of the Spirit. But how can we love in the power of the Spirit if we do not possess His fullness? Only through this power to love given us by the Spirit possessed in fullness do we begin to love each other as Jesus loved us.

To love thus in the power of the Spirit, however, does not make the observance of this new commandment easy. Jesus taught that "a servant is not greater than his master" (Jn. 15:20). Life in the fullness of the Spirit does not take away the necessity of suffering. But, in the fullness of the Spirit, loving as Jesus loved becomes possible. In the fullness of the Spirit we are empowered to love. In that power we learn how to remain open to the leading of the Spirit. Because of our freedom we can easily fall short of loving as Jesus did. But through a life in the fullness of the Spirit we gradually come to such an openness and surrender to Jesus that we begin in His power to love as He loved.

To learn to love as Jesus loved takes time. Often a healing needs to take place before a Christian baptized in the Spirit can co-operate with the Spirit's power to love. People can be merciless in demanding of Christians newly baptized in the Spirit an immediate radical change. This is not the mind of Jesus. He is a gracious and considerate Lord. He accomplishes His will *in time*. The gift of His grace is always given in time. Jesus knows that learning to love takes time. If we love each other as He loves us, we will also give each other the time necessary to learn to love as He loves.

## The Testing Ground of Community

A Spirit-filled Christian should be easily recognized by the fruit his life bears. St. Paul leaves us in no doubt as to what fruit the Spirit-filled Christian in due time is to bear:

> What the Spirit brings is very different: love, joy, peace, patience, kindness, goodness, trustfulness, gentleness and self-control. [Ga. 5:22–23.]

What a tapestry of life the Spirit can weave with these qualities
when given free reign in the life of the believer! The Spirit-filled
Christian becomes empowered with all these qualities in all in-
terpersonal relationships.

However, there remains a testing ground, community life, to
authenticate the grace of the fullness of the Spirit. Living for a
sufficient length of time in community is the only way to prove
that one has received the Spirit in fullness. One need but look at
married couples, at religious, or at the single person: If these are
bearing the fruits of the Spirit in their respective community life,
then we know the Lord Jesus has gifted them with the fullness
of His Spirit.

The love expected by Jesus of His followers to whom He has
given His Spirit in fullness is described by Paul:

> Love is always patient and kind; it is never jealous; love is never
> boastful or conceited; it is never rude or selfish; it does not take
> offense, and is not resentful. Love takes no pleasure in other peo-
> ple's sins but delights in the truth; it is always ready to excuse, to
> trust, to hope, and to endure whatever comes. Loves does not
> come to an end. [1 Co. 13:4–8.]

The Spirit enabled Jesus to love. It is impossible for us to love
each other as Jesus has loved us unless we have that Spirit given
to us in fullness. Neither human nature nor even the un-
developed grace of Baptism confers on us the power to love as
we ought. For this power we need a full awakening of the grace
of Confirmation, a grace ever renewed and developed by the
grace of the Eucharist.

Since we are to love each other as Jesus has loved us, we turn
to Him as the only example for us of this love. An incident that
describes His love is His conduct at the Last Supper. John the
Evangelist, His friend, understands this behavior of Jesus:

> He had always loved those who were his in the world, but now
> he showed how perfect his love was. [Jn. 13:1b.]

The perfection of His love is shown first in His act of washing
the disciples' feet. Then John recounts the prediction by Jesus of

His betrayal by Judas. The prediction stunned the apostles so much that they wanted Jesus to identify the betrayer. Jesus did so in a very subtle way.

It was the custom for the host at a Jewish meal to give a choice morsel to an honored guest.

> "It is the one . . . to whom I give the piece of bread that I shall dip in the dish." [Jn. 13:26.]

To share bread was to pledge fidelity. It was saying in effect: I will rather be broken in body as this bread is broken, I will rather be consumed as this bread is eaten, than allow our friendship to be betrayed. The reaction of Jesus to His betrayal by Judas was to extend to him the covenant of eternal love and friendship. Jesus truly loved Judas "to the very end." This fidelity and love should have been for Judas the beginning of a new relationship with Jesus. Instead, Judas ruptures His relationship with Jesus completely.

> At that instant, after Judas had taken the bread, Satan entered him. [Jn. 13:27.]

Jesus at the Last Supper, even though He knew Judas was intending to betray Him, was

> ready to excuse, to trust, to hope, and to endure whatever comes. [1 Co. 13:7.]

Jesus *could* love this way because He had such power to love from the Spirit of His Father.

## He Was Humbler Yet

The fullness of the Spirit is indeed manifested through faith and love. But there is a third way in which the fullness of the Spirit should authenticate itself in the life of the Christian: by humility. Humility is the human response of Jesus, the man, to the way in which the Spirit had the Son of God assume a human nature:

He did not cling
to his equality with God
but emptied himself
to assume the condition of a slave,
and became as men are;
and being as all men are,
he was humbler yet,
even to accepting death,
death on a cross.
[Ph. 2:6–8.]

This text suggests that no man has ever been, or will ever be, more humble than Jesus. This humility was not a play-acting by Jesus. It was an expression of His "in the Spirit" relationship with all people. Through the light of the Spirit Jesus saw Himself as their slave. The Spirit made Him aware He was the Savior, the Messiah, the Christ. But the Spirit also drove Him to a life of humble, even menial, service. Jewish custom reserved the act of foot-washing for slaves. The apostles accordingly did not think of performing this act. Jesus was the one who thought of it and who voluntarily did it. He felt He was unworthy of doing even this. It was not too much for Him to do for them. For He was their slave, all the more so because He was the Christ and the Messiah.

This humility prompted Jesus to live totally for others. He lived first of all for His Father. This humility disposed Him to follow the guidance of the Spirit. Hence Jesus *heard* the Father speak to Him and He was impelled to heed the word He heard:

The Lord Yahweh has given me
a disciple's tongue.
So that I may know how to reply to the wearied
he provides me with speech.
Each morning he wakes me to hear,
to listen like a disciple.
The Lord Yahweh has opened my ear.
[Is. 50:4.]

These words of Isaiah were true primarily of Jesus. They bore fruit in His life of obedience to the Father. "My food is to do the

will of the one who sent me" (Jn. 4:34). His humility before the
Father expressed itself also in a life of prayer, first in the prayer
of praise but also in earnest petition. If Jesus had not been as
humble as He was, He would not have withdrawn so frequently
from the crowds to be in communion with His Father.

Jesus did not live for Himself. There was not a tinge of
selfishness in Him. The Father's will consumed Him entirely. For
this reason Jesus was able to love others as He did. The Spirit,
working through His gift of humility, kept Jesus free of all self-
indulgence. The words which Paul would later write to the Galatians describe the humility of Jesus:

> Let me put it like this: if you are guided by the Spirit you will be
> in no danger of yielding to self-indulgence, since self-indulgence
> is the opposite of the Spirit; the Spirit is totally against such a
> thing, and it is precisely because the two are so opposed that you
> do not always carry out your good intentions. If you are led by
> the Spirit, no law can touch you. [Ga. 5:16–18.]

Jesus was always led totally by the Spirit. The Spirit was His
life; therefore, He was directed by the Spirit (Ga. 5:25). There
is no other way of explaining His profound humility, which bore
fruit in such self-sacrificing love and charity. Never did He seek
His own glory. Never did He glory in self-esteem. His heart
burned with a profound respect for the dignity of every man, especially for the lowly ones, the poor, women, children, and even
more so, for sinners. Human respect could not touch Him. He
was truly free—from self. He was truly the humblest of men. In
His humility the Spirit shone forth.

"Learn from me, for I am gentle and humble in heart" (Mt.
11:29). The Spirit of Jesus given in fullness imparts the humility
of Christ. The Spirit makes the Christian humble before *all* men.
Such humility will be an authentic sign of the Spirit present in
the Christian who claims to have received Him in fullness.

There are other manifestations of the Spirit in fullness. All of
them are important. All have their proper place and function.
The charisms mentioned by Paul in 1 Corinthians 12 are of special importance. They all manifest the Spirit acting in power

through a Christian for the upholding of the Body. Our concern has not been to describe the operation of these charisms. Our concern has rather been to describe the *ongoing life* of the Christian baptized in the Spirit. The classical charisms of the Spirit are, in their operation at least, transient gifts of power. But the Spirit is the gift of Jesus who abides:

"I shall ask the Father,
and he will give you another Advocate
to be with you for ever. . . .
he is with you, he is in you."
[Jn. 14:16–17.]

His abiding presence in fullness needs to have its own manifestations. Of these we have mentioned three: faith, love, humility. Through these the Spirit unites the Christian most intimately with Jesus, enabling the person to bear witness authentically to Jesus as the Savior, the Christ, and the Lord:

"When the Advocate comes,
whom I shall send to you from the Father,
the Spirit of truth who issues from the Father,
he will be my witness.
And you too will be witnesses,
because you have been with me from the outset."
[Jn. 15:26–27.]

In this chapter I have indicated a few of the basic manifestations of the grace of the fullness of the Spirit in the life of a Christian. This was done not merely to show how important is this grace but also to point out the many and varied forms in which the Spirit manifests Himself. Fullness in the Spirit is neither the fancy nor the luxury of a few. It is necessary for all confirmed Christians. It is no accidental or superficial adornment. It is essential to the very life of a Christian.

The grace of the fullness in the Holy Spirit has as many different manifestations as there are persons. This book is the story of the manifestations I have experienced through encountering the Spirit. The process of these ongoing manifestations of the Spirit—and their essential role in our life—will be unique in the life of each Christian. Since there is an order and priority among them, there is the need to understand the place and purpose of each.

These manifestations of the Spirit's presence can be grouped into various categories. There are the three great theological virtues of faith, hope, and love; there are the moral and infused virtues; there are the traditional seven "gifts" of the Holy Spirit; there are the fruits of the presence of the Spirit; and finally, there are the many charisms of the Holy Spirit of which Scripture and the Fathers of the Church speak. All of these are realities of the Spirit at work in the life of a Christian.

To live in the Spirit, however, does mean one essential thing: to live under the Lordship of Jesus. Jesus is Lord! Jesus is my Lord, and Jesus is your Lord. This is our common faith as Christians. This is our exultant hymn of praise, and in a real sense this is the simplest and most profound article of our faith. God's people of old had a similar profession of faith and hymn of praise. It is still the article of faith for the Jewish people of today—the cornerstone of their prayer, both public and private: "Listen, Israel: Yahweh our God is the one Yahweh" (Dt. 6:4).

Jesus Himself said that He did not come to abolish the Law and the Prophets but to fulfill them (Mt. 5:17). The Law and the Prophets proclaim the Lordship of Israel's God, but Jesus brings their word to its fullness by becoming the Lord, Who is God. As the prophets of old called the people to listen, to hear their God, and to proclaim Him as their Lord, so now the Father Himself calls out to all of us, His children, saying to us:

"This is my Son, the Chosen One. Listen to him." [Lk. 9:35.]

U-7